"Danielle Strickland unpicks centu— —
the status of women in the church
striking and refreshing."
   – **David Westlake,** Integral N

"Read The Liberating Truth *and a*
the heart of God that will rock your w—. Danielle is a true
ambassador for the Kingdom of God. She is a hard core lover of
Jesus and has been powerfully used by God. I deeply love, respect,
and fully endorse Danielle Strickland."
   – **Patricia King,** Co-Founder of XPmedia

"This may be the most significant issue of our time – a Christ-
saturated view of gender – specifically, how Jesus sees females, and
what the Bible actually says about it. In our lifetime millions
of women and girls are being trafficked and millions of female
babies have been aborted. Within the church countless women
with Holy Spirit gifts and callings to preach the Gospel and to
lead, have been silenced, marginalised and disempowered. The
need for the insights expressed in this book is urgent!"
   – **Lieut.-Colonel Janet Munn,** Secretary for Spiritual Life
   Development, The Salvation Army

"This book is amazing! Danielle gives us the theology of how
God views women and specifically how this relates to women in
leadership. It is an incredibly practical guide on what it takes to
be in leadership and how to reach your potential. I'm delighted
that Danielle has written this book. She's the living embodiment
of its message and one of the most inspiring people I know!"
   – **Wendy Beech-Ward,** Director, Spring Harvest

"Danielle's passion for the Kingdom of God shines through
as she champions God's agenda for freedom and equality. A
challenging and powerful read for both sexes."
   – **Mike Pilavachi,** Soul Survivor

"The Liberating Truth *is just that: liberating and truth! Danielle Strickland is one of the most anointed communicators I have ever heard. These pages will keep you gripped, challenge you, open you up to truth-filled revelation and empower you.*"

– **Faytene Kryskow,** Author/Revivalist, TheCRY and MY Canada

"*If you want to change the world, empower women – it is as true now as it has always been. In a world where the ugly and dangerous prejudice of gender discrimination is still too often disguised by an appeal to doctrinal correctness,* The Liberating Truth *poses a profound challenge.*"

– **Steve Chalke MBE,** UN Special Advisor on Community Action Against Human Trafficking

"*I am a woman and I want my life to make a difference. I am a leader who wants to know that God is leading me. I have a daughter who will know that God calls women to take a lead in making the world a different place. Danielle reminds us that God liberates us all from the limitations of this world.*"

– **Ruth Dearnley,** Chief Executive, Stop the Traffik

"*God has always used women on the frontline. Too often they've been prevented from taking their place by their own misgivings, by the prejudice and injustice of male leaders setting restrictions, or discriminatory cultural norms.*

"*Reading this book will convince you to let God have his way, unfettered, so that women, empowered by the Holy Spirit, take their place to preach, to lead, and influence the growth of God's Kingdom. This book gives timely, forceful, passionate support from every angle – biblically and theologically, socially and culturally, historically and politically, and especially spiritually from a Jesus perspective.*

"*Danielle Strickland not only convinces in word, but to see her in action and hear her preach is living proof of God's power through an obedient servant.*"

– **General Dr Eva Burrows,** The Salvation Army

The Liberating Truth

How Jesus Empowers Women

Danielle Strickland

MONARCH
BOOKS
Oxford, UK & Grand Rapids, Michigan, USA

First published in the UK in 2011 by Monarch Books (a publishing imprint of Lion Hudson plc) and by Elevation (a publishing imprint of the Memralife Group):

Lion Hudson plc, Wilkinson House, Jordan Hill Road, Oxford OX2 8DR
Tel: +44 (0)1865 302750; Fax +44 (0)1865 302757;
email monarch@lionhudson.com; www.lionhudson.com
Memralife Group, 14 Horsted Square, Uckfield, East Sussex TN22 1QG
Tel: +44 (0)1825 746530; Fax +44 (0)1825 748899;
www.elevationmusic.com

ISBN 978 0 85721 019 7 (print)
ISBN 978 0 85721 106 4 (ePub)
ISBN 978 0 85721 105 7 (Kindle)
ISBN 978 0 85721 107 1 (PDF)

Distributed by:
UK: Marston Book Services, PO Box 269, Abingdon, Oxon, OX14 4YN
USA: Kregel Publications, PO Box 2607, Grand Rapids, Michigan 49501

Acknowledgments – see page 159

The text paper used in this book has been made from wood independently certified as having come from sustainable forests.

British Library Cataloguing Data
A catalogue record for this book is available from the British Library.

Printed and bound in Great Britain by Clays Ltd, St Ives plc.

Contents

"In the nineteenth century, the central moral challenge was slavery. In the twentieth century, it was the battle against totalitarianism. We believe that in this century the paramount moral challenge will be the struggle for gender equality around the world."

Half the Sky: How to Change the World,
Nicholas D. Kristof and Sheryl WuDunn (Virago, 2010)

Dedication

This book is dedicated to the women who, in the midst of prejudice and persecution, have paved the way towards living a love that liberates. This empowering truth has changed my life and offers the kind of hope that I'm convinced will change the world.

To my husband and co-labourer in the fight for God's kingdom come: your life is empowering; your love like a blazing fire; like a mighty flame. I'm living my best life with you. What joy.

To my two boys, Zion and Judah: you were born to change the world and you've already begun with me. You are warriors; may these truths help liberate you to fight by living a better way.

Acknowledgments

Vicky – you are a legend! Wendy – you are great with a pencil! Thanks to Caroline, Tony and Jenny (and all those at Lion Hudson). Thanks to all those denominations and church organizations who are willing to stand up with and for women. Here's to God's kingdom come! To the women in whose wake I walk – thank you. And to all the godly men I know who walk in this great revelation and make God look good – thank you.

Foreword

I felt a tap on my shoulder. I'd just led worship for a group of pastors who were having a regional gathering for their denomination. I'd set off that morning, looking forward to singing and praying for our part of the United States. My sense of discomfort began when one of the pastors arrived and said "Wow, they've asked *you* to lead worship?" I didn't really understand why he had said that, until I came out from backstage, and saw there was not one woman present in the auditorium, except for two quiet females at the back who were making tea and coffee.

This denomination believes that only men can be called to be pastors. If a woman takes a job in one of their churches, even though the job description is the same, a man would receive the title "pastor", but the woman would be called "director". A woman would, I was told, frequently be paid about half what a man would be paid for the same position, as the denomination consider men to be the primary breadwinners in a household.

When I heard I was leading worship for the regional pastor's gathering, I should have logged the fact that I would be standing as a lone female in a large room full

11

of guys, some of whom probably didn't think I should be standing on a stage.

Brushing this aside, I led a time of sung worship and then read from Isaiah to set up the final song. I saw a few men raise their eyebrows at the sight of me on stage, speaking with a Bible in my hand. I felt like that would be the low point of my morning, but I was wrong.

I put down my guitar, and was excited to join these men in praying for our city. Walking down from the stage, I took the one empty seat left in the room as one of the leaders invited us to stand and begin praying. That was when someone tapped me on the shoulder.

"Vicky, can I have a quick word with you outside?" It was one of the pastors from the church. It seemed a bizarre time to want to chat, when we were about to dive into praying for revival – something that is dear to my heart.

Seeing the somewhat urgent look in his eyes, I followed him out, walking past all the men and then standing outside. The pastor leaned his arm across the door to the auditorium in a relaxed but "you can't get back in there" kind of manner. I felt increasingly uncomfortable as I began to add things up in my head.

He stumbled through some random and seemingly meaningless chatter. "How are you? How's your week going?" This was getting weirder by the moment.

"Great to chat," I said with a smile, "but I came to pray for revival today, so I'd like to get back in and be part of that if you don't mind…"

"Err, I can't let you back in there," he said awkwardly.

"How come?" I asked, confused.

"Because you're a woman," he replied.

I tried not to react, hoping my eyes weren't welling up, and my cheeks weren't turning pink. I didn't want him to see how much this was hurting and shocking me.

"This is a pastor's prayer meeting. You can't be a pastor because you're female, so I can't let you back in. It would just cause too much trouble, too many ripples. But feel free to come back and join us for lunch…"

His voice trailed off as he saw me backing away down the hallway. I didn't say a word. I just left quietly. I couldn't believe this kind of gender discrimination still existed in Christian circles.

Some people don't ever feel aware of their gender in relation to their calling, but I can say that I've felt extremely aware of it in all the twelve years I've been in ministry. Twice I've been on the staff of churches that firmly believed women should not be allowed to preach or teach. Both places made me feel second-class, like somehow I couldn't be taken as seriously as the men – like somehow I'd misheard that God was calling me to communicate His Word. It took a lot of my confidence away and only through prayer and counselling have I recovered my belief that God has indeed called me to lead, speak, and pastor for Him.

I'm now living in England and am surprised to find that several major church movements here also believe that women can't be elders or senior church leaders. Why is this damaging theology so prevalent? Having studied it in depth at the University of Oxford during my theology degree, I find it incredible that so many people really believe that the Bible outlines these things. Jesus was pro-women, pro-equality, pro-love. I long for the church to reflect this!

I've channelled my disappointment and pain about these things into serving the church and trying to be a visual testimony to younger girls and women that they *can* sing, preach, travel, minister, and pastor. I encourage them to rise up and be all that God has called them to be. If you are one of the many women across the globe who has found me and poured out your painful story about feeling second-class within God's family, I salute you for your patience, and I'm cheering you on as you continue to run the race. Jesus is the example to follow. He was gracious and loving, but also truthful, honest, and clear. Don't be a doormat, or remain in a situation where you are being damaged, but whatever you do, do it with the loving attitude of Jesus.

I rarely talk about this kind of stuff, as it seems divisive. But I feel the time has come to talk openly, to shine light on the problems that exist so that we can try and fix them for the women who are stuck in these situations. If we change our systems and structures and begin to encourage and affirm women, hopefully the younger generation won't have to experience the same things many of us have gone through. The book you are about to read will be a great catalyst and a fire-starter in this process.

Meeting Danielle Strickland was a breath of fresh air and a moment of great hope for me. She embodies the same DNA, longing to see women released into their callings. She's a freedom fighter, blazing a trail with her lifestyle and message.

Danielle is not just a fantastic "female speaker", but she is a fantastic speaker and communicator, *period*. She stands comfortably next to any communicator of our day, and delivers a compelling message with amazing ease and power. She is also extremely down to earth and hilarious, which I love. Tattooed, unassuming, and probably just back from a trip taking cupcakes to a local brothel, Danielle is a living example of Jesus.

She chooses to live with the poor and the outcast, basing herself in areas of cities that most people avoid. She's a major in the Salvation Army, yet she is completely without ego. It's clear to me why prostitutes, addicts, and the forgotten poor adore her company. Few people are as genuine, raw, and kind as she is – it draws people in and makes them feel at home. It reminds me of someone else who hung out a lot with outcasts, lepers, and thieves – Jesus.

I am delighted to commend this book to you. May God use this book to raise up thousands of girls and women with Danielle's passion, vision, and heart for justice. May the light of this book break into the darkness like a beacon, lifting up the weary heads of women who feel on the sidelines. And may men read this book, and know that we deeply love and respect them. May we all stand shoulder-to-shoulder and heart to heart, as the male and female equals that God intended us to be; a united army of Jesus-lovers, gazing on his beauty and changing the world with his love.

Vicky Beeching
England, 2010
www.vickybeeching.com

Part One

Brothels and Burqas

CHAPTER ONE

You are Not a Princess

A few years ago I read a popular Christian book written for women. It was highly recommended by a friend who told me it had changed her life. I thought it'd be worth a read. I liked the book in many ways. I think I understood what the authors were trying to say, but, to be honest, it really bothered me at the same time.

It troubled me because it contained every possible feminine cliché known to humanity. It bothered me because it assumed that a woman's longing for a man to complete her was gospel truth instead of an enemy lie. It smothered me in gooey princess talk that made me think I'd been invited to a pyjama party hosted by the Spice Girls.

Its premise was that every little girl longs to be a princess. Now, I know that tons of little girls do long to be princesses. All the more, I'm sure, because we help them along with excessive cultural clues. But it concerned me because I didn't fit with that norm. I didn't match the recipe. I couldn't relate.

I called my mother to ask if I had actually once longed to be a princess but then stuffed my feelings down and repressed them because of something terrible and tragic that had happened that distorted my feminine state. I was starting to think that I might never have had what it takes to be a true woman. After all, in this book my wholeness and salvation were rooted in the fact that I should have a female need to be a princess.

My mother laughed out loud. She said that I had never once even hinted that I had a longing or a need or a desire to be a princess. She was still laughing when she reminded me of the number of times she offered me money to wear a dress and I couldn't be convinced. She laughed because now, years later, as a wife and mother in full-time ministry, emotionally healthy and strongly independent, I was letting a popular Christian book bother me so much. But it did.

The popular Christian concept of a "good woman" is someone extremely feminine, sensitive, good-looking, and submissive to a handsome husband who keeps his promises. Lovely – if you live in Disneyland. Or, actually, if you live in this male-dominated, externally obsessed Western world.

I think that's the thing that concerns me the most: the Christian woman looks just like the Oprah one. Glossy magazines, enhanced body parts, and Botox for everyone.

So – teeth whitening and skinny jeans make for a satisfied Christian life?

Where is that in the Bible?

And is God's plan for me really about squeezing myself into a worldly mode where I'm judged by my external self before my internal self has a chance to breathe? I mean, I've even heard of female Christian worship leaders being critiqued on their size and appearance. Whatever happened to talent and gifting and anointing?

N. T. Wright wrote about this stereotyping: "When you look at strip cartoons, B grade movies, and Z grade novels and poems, you pick up a standard view of how 'everyone imagines' men and women behave. Men are macho, loud-mouthed, arrogant thugs, always fighting and wanting their own way. Women are simpering, empty-headed creatures with nothing to think about except clothes and jewellery. There are Christian versions of this, too: the men must make the decisions, run the show, always be in the lead, tell everyone what to do; women must stay at home and bring up the children."[1]

In my real world – God's intended one – it doesn't line up that every female has the same feelings or desires or hopes or dreams.

We aren't prototypes.

21

We are people.

We're all different. Unique. We have a plethora of dreams and hopes and desires, all rooted in God's great plan for the world to be changed.

Each of us is invited to be part of this global agenda. We all have a role.

Gender-based restrictions are simply old-fashioned and unhelpful tools that do much more harm than good. They need to be done away with, not simply because they contribute to the dissatisfaction of both men and women, but also because they limit the people of God. In the fullness of God's kingdom, real relationships should be based on dignity and equality, not on gender and difference.

This isn't limited to women, of course. The enemy's strategy of gender-based restrictions also extends to men and to marriage.

One of my most difficult moments as a church leader came when I had to ask a visiting teaching group to leave after their first presentation at a marriage seminar weekend. I simply couldn't let them continue. Their whole concept of a good marriage was based on gender-specific roles. In other words, women, because they are more inclined towards service, ought to take care of the house; and men, because they are more inclined towards economics, should take care of the finances... This went on for a while. I looked around at the couples who filled the hall in our small town. Even a quick overview of the crowd completely smashed their theory. Across the hall from me was a bloke who was a clean freak; his wife was an accountant.

I know of couples who strive after the "perfect marriage" where the woman does specific things because she's the woman and the man does certain things because he's the man – and everyone is so busy and so desperate to fit the grid of a perfect life that they miss the real one. They miss God's celebration of diversity – the lovely, colour-filled spectrum of people of all shapes and sizes and conditions. Some single, some married, some divorced; some tall, others round; some broken and some not so much. Some are independent and fierce and others are sensitive and caring – and all of them are invited to change the world.

All of them. Yes, even the skinny, perfect-looking, happily married, smiley ones with extra-white teeth!

So this book is a celebration of the diversity of God's calling to all people. What I know for sure is that nothing is locked in – the invitation is wide open. He wants you to contribute any way you can. You are *not* limited to gender-based work or children's work, or emotionally sensitive pastoral work. You are invited to any work you feel called to do and are equipped to undertake. You are invited into a kingdom that knows no distinction between Greek or Jew or black or white or male or female... we are all one in Christ Jesus (Galatians 3:28).

The differences, the divides, the restraints have been removed. We can move forward, in abandoned surrender, in order to bring God's kingdom to earth as it is in heaven.

I have a hunch that heaven is full of fat, skinny, tall, short, black, brown, white and maybe even blue folks – our perfection comes in our surrender to God and his purposes for us, not in the sameness of identikit lives.

You are not a princess. You are a person. And that is good news.

CHAPTER TWO

Killing Us with Cotton

You can now buy Barbie wearing a burqa.

So, if you're tired of young women constantly being taught that it's more important to look good than to be good, and tired of seeing skimpy clothing on disproportionate dolls that make young girls dissatisfied with their own real, healthy bodies – cheer up. You can now buy a doll that's completely covered, from head to toe, in a different kind of oppression. What a liberated world.

Women can't seem to catch a break in this culture. On one hand we're told by some people – neo-feminists who have hijacked equality to mean equal oppression for all – that our best bet is to use our bodies and our sexuality to cash in on economic prosperity. Proponents of this philosophy say it with a straight face. They write about it in magazines and in movie scripts and sing about it at rock concerts. Pop singers like Lady Gaga will have you literally tied up in bondage as you sing about your freedom.

All of this is done in the name of liberation.

On the other hand, some Muslim extremists suggest that wearing a burqa – covering your whole body, from head to toe – is liberating for women.

An interesting symbol of freedom.

The problem is that no matter how you dress up oppression, it will never lead to freedom.

I met a young Muslim girl on a flight from Cape Town, South Africa, to Zambia after an excruciatingly long journey from the other side of the world. When she joined the plane she came in with an entourage of five other Islamic women, all dressed from head to toe in black with only a small eye slit open so that they could see. The rest of the group headed to the back of the plane but the young girl's seat was next to mine, right at the front. When I get overtired I get a little hyper, so when she sat down and had her seat belt on, I made my move. Most likely it was out of sheer boredom, but before I thought too much about our differences, I leaned way over so I was in her line of sight, waved my hand in a friendly gesture and said "Hello". As you do.

She was a bit surprised but she said hello back and a conversation began.

All the niceties followed: "Where are you from?", "Where are you going?"…

It turned out she was just finishing her Islamic studies at a school where her father was the principal. She said she'd had to leave to help take care of her cousins while her brother was on a mission. Feeling a bit awkward about finding out what kind of mission this might be (it was only shortly after the 9/11 attacks), I tried a different line of conversation. "What are your favourite subjects at school?"

She answered, "Evangelism."

What?

She explained that many of her Christian friends had converted to Islam. Once they understood the realities of her faith they were ready to accept it and join her. She was a gifted evangelist.

I was intrigued and told her to give her evangelism strategy a go on me. She was delighted and took off into a long monologue about the nobility of pursing a holy life, the covering of a burqa, the camaraderie of women in Islam, how good it was to be protected from people viewing her as a sexual object, etc…

I was amazed. I knew enough about the Muslim faith to know that it's hard work at best, and at worst an oppressive religion that hopes for salvation through works – an impossibility. No matter how good you are, you can never be good enough without Jesus. This is just basic math.

After she had finished, she was kind and polite enough to ask me about my faith. Now I had a chance to tell her all the basic fundamental doctrines, the top ten reasons why I believe Christianity is a better faith than Islam. But for some reason, I sensed the promptings of God to tell her about my relationship with Jesus.

I explained that I had encountered Jesus when I didn't deserve mercy or love and He had given salvation to me as a gift. I began to follow Him, I said, because I had never known such mercy, grace, and love in my whole life – and I wanted to be like Him. I told her that I was impressed with her presentation of her faith, but, as enticing as it seemed, I could never imagine my life without Jesus.

Silence.

I thought I'd offended her. I thought I'd been too overpowering. I wondered if I'd taken things too far – maybe she'd get into trouble because she'd listened to me? I sat there, and, to stop my fear-based worrying, I just prayed.

And waited.

Finally, she turned to me, looked me in the eye and said some very powerful words. "Would you like to see my face?"

Wow.

I guess the question we all need to hear from women all over the globe is the same. We know that cultural divides are huge. We know that the deep injustices against women across the world and in the church seem almost insurmountable. But the real question – the question Jesus is keen to hear, and the question that has the power to change things – is one of intimacy, relationship, and connection. It has emotional power and a bonding value. It can connect us in ways we can only imagine.

"Would you like to see my face?"

I responded with a resounding "Yes!" As a matter of fact, I felt a holy shiver of privilege and tension and gave a nervous glance over my shoulder in case her entourage was hovering anywhere near our seats. Then I sat there as she pulled back her burqa and showed me who she was.

And my friend Asma was beautiful. Sixteen years old beautiful, with big dimples, mischievous eyes, and a huge smile that lit up her whole face. She was so lovely it's hard to describe.

And then Asma asked me another question. "Am I what you expected?"

And the answer to that question was "No." She wasn't anything like I had imagined her to be. She was beyond all my thoughts. She was different in every good way. She was so lovely. So beautiful. So joyful. Unique.

I've found that this is true about women everywhere. I've met some amazing women, in brothels and in burqas, in tragic circumstances and under crushing oppression. But they have all been overflowing with potential and life. Their faces are full of beauty, worth, value, dignity, and joy, and this gives me great hope for the future.

I guess the question I'm really hoping to ask you in

this book is: Are you willing to look beyond the issues of gender injustice, past prejudices, church politics, and the imbalances of power, and to see their faces? The real faces of women meeting the true heart of God.

This is where true power and beauty lies.

❂ ❂ ❂

Although Asma told me that wearing her burqa meant she didn't have to worry about being judged or gawked at because of how she looked, other Islamic women compare wearing the burqa to a jail sentence.

For Faranooz Nazir, the world all but vanished beneath the tent-like covering of her burqa. Its thick mesh panel limited her vision, her movement, and the air she breathed. "I couldn't hear. I couldn't see. I couldn't walk", she says. "It was as if the world no longer existed to me and I no longer existed to the world." She now refuses to wear the full veil.

The Revolutionary Association of Women of Afghanistan (RAWA), based in Pakistan, calls being forced to wear a burqa "killing us with cotton". The group says that forcing women to wear the burqa is one of the ways the Taliban has taken Islamic law – or *sharia* – to its utmost extreme. Debbie Howlett wrote in *USA Today*: "While the Taliban has outlawed keeping birds trapped in cages, it has barred Afghan women from leaving their houses. Women cannot work, attend school, or receive treatment from a male doctor. They are forbidden to show an ankle or even make a noise with their shoes – the sound of which is considered too tempting for men to resist. Offenders are beaten, in some cases to death." [1]

And the burqa has become a much-contested issue in democratic nations with Muslim immigrants, including Canada, where I live. In the Canadian province of Quebec the full-face burqa has been legally banned when the wearer has any interaction with a government or tax-funded programme. The idea behind the ban is simple: we need to see each other's faces.

Part of the rationale behind the ban was explained in an article in the Canadian newspaper, *National Post*:

> For those…who instinctively hate the niqab but feel guilty about banning it, it will help them if they understand that the burqa and niqab are not "worn," but "borne". The niqab is not an article of clothing; it is a tent-like piece of cloth supplemental to clothing. Full cover is worn as a reminder to the "bearer" that she is not free, and to remind the observer that the bearer is a possession, something less than a full human being.
>
> The question of full coverage is therefore not one of tolerance, or rights, or choice, or freedom of expression. It is a question of social and civic propriety. No citizen can be said to be free if they cannot exchange a smile with their fellow citizens. And no citizen can be psychologically comfortable

sharing public space with other citizens who refuse to be seen.

It is no use pretending fully covered women do no harm to the social fabric. They arouse internal disturbance in others: a mixture of self-consciousness, pity, guilt, fear and resentment, the last because in any encounter with them we feel shunned, and cannot "read" their expression, which is a necessity for both social and security reasons.[2]

When I lived in Australia it was considered somewhat politically incorrect to challenge the cultural norm of prostitution. In recent days around the world it has become politically incorrect to challenge the wearing of the burqa and the realities of the lives of women who live every day under oppressive Muslim regimes. The harsh injustices they face always seem to be described as "cultural realities".

As a matter of fact, the main idea this rhetoric supposes is that it's not only none of my business, but I should stop judging other cultures and leave them alone. This is an interesting theory for sure. Why is it that "cultural realities" are only to be respected when it comes to the oppression of women? If the "cultural reality" is cannibalism, then we challenge it. If it's murder or child sacrifice, we challenge it. If it's terrorism, we spend trillions of dollars to combat it.

But if it's the oppression of girls and women, then we excuse it as a "cultural difference". This is absurd and needs to stop. I do believe that all cultures are different and need to be respected, even learned from, but to think that the oppression of women in any culture anywhere should be tolerated and respected is a great travesty that will be used as judgment on us later. The harsh realities of gender-based violence and crime around the world must be challenged – in every culture.

Aisha's story is so appalling that it hit the headlines worldwide (cover story, *Time* magazine, Thursday 29 July 2010). Aisha ran away from her husband's house at the age of 18. Her in-laws had beaten her and treated her like a slave. Fearing for her life, she had fled. One night members of the local Taliban militia surrounded the house in the village in the southern Afghan province of Uruzgan where she had taken refuge. They dragged her to a nearby mountain clearing, where she had to face the blinding flashlights of her husband's family. Ignoring her pleas, the local Taliban commander ordered her to be punished, as an example to other girls. Aisha's brother-in-law held her down while her husband approached with a knife, slicing off first her ears and then her nose. The men left her lying there in the cold air to die.

Aisha passed out from the pain, but came to later, choking on her own blood. Through her own courage and the compassion of brave neighbours, she survived to describe what had happened. This is a story not from fifty years ago, or even ten: it is from present-day Afghanistan.

Aisha's family did nothing to protect her from the Taliban. That might have been out of fear, but more likely it was out of shame. A girl who runs away is automatically considered a prostitute in deeply traditional societies, and a family that allowed her back home would be subject to widespread ridicule. In rural areas, a family that finds itself shamed by a daughter sometimes sells her into slavery, or subjects her to a so-called honour killing – murder under the guise of saving the family's name.

Aisha survived and found her way to a shelter, but her father tried to bring her home, promising that he would find her a new husband. Aisha refused to go.

It's time to stop excusing terrible behaviour as a cultural norm and to start challenging it so that it becomes a rare event rather than a daily reality for the people – mostly women – who suffer under it.

And it can be done. Seismic changes in attitudes can happen.

❧ ❧ ❧

The authors of the landmark book on women and global injustice, *Half the Sky* point out that

> Honour killings, sexual slavery, and genital cutting may seem to Western readers to be tragic but inevitable in a world far, far away. In much the same way, slavery was once widely viewed by many decent Europeans and Americans as a regrettable

but ineluctable feature of human life. It was just one more horror that had existed for thousands of years. But then in the 1780s a few indignant Britons, led by William Wilberforce, decided that slavery was so offensive that they had to abolish it. And they did. Today we see the seed of something similar: a global movement to emancipate women and girls.[3]

Under some of the cultural norms that people are frightened of challenging, women are scared to jeopardize their marriages or damage their husbands' egos by taking up leadership posts. Young girls "dumb down" in order to catch a good-looking guy, because they've been encouraged to believe that men want their girls simple. Others continue to replicate sexual oppression as a lifestyle of "freedom" at the expense of inner security, confidence, and a healthy sense of self.

Recently I heard a talk about the biblical King David and his terrible behaviour around Bathsheba and her husband Uriah. David watched Bathsheba taking a bath, and lusted after her. So he arranged for her husband, Uriah, to be killed, apparently accidentally, in battle. The talk I heard helped to explain King David's actions by drawing a parallel between his attitude and our contemporary fixation with possessing things. The speaker suggested that the dominant theme of our culture used to be an attitude of appreciation. We would go to museums or to art galleries or to a neighbour's house and appreciate beauty and wisdom and everything that was lovely. We could even touch the lovely things and look at them and marvel – then put them back and walk away.

Nowadays, this is no longer the case.

Today, in the West, our culture tries to persuade us not to appreciate things or people or gadgets or status, but to possess them. We want to own everything we see – not just appreciate it. This is what the Bible means by "lusting after" something. We often only use the word "lust" in the context of sexuality, but it actually has a wider meaning. The constant, nagging longing to possess the lovely things before our eyes does something deeply dangerous to our souls.

In recent generations, women have been overwhelmed by a consumer culture that believes that women can be owned and "had" rather than appreciated and respected. This culture continues to rise up against women and girls, suggesting that they be controlled, dominated and exploited for no reason other than that they belong to the "wrong" gender.

It's time the liberating truth hit the news – God intends something much better for us. So, whether it's head-to-toe cotton symbolizing our bondage and silence or whether it's bikinis and Botox and depression and self-hatred – an emotional cotton of touch-ups and impossibilities – we will not let cotton kill us.

CHAPTER THREE

A Song of Lies

I spent the better part of a year in Russia right after the collapse of the Soviet Union. It was a mess. The Iron Curtain's veneer of strength and power was revealed as a complete crock. A total lie. It was, well, rather embarrassing.

One of the things I was privileged to do while I was there was run a camp for kids. We held it in an old Soviet-era pioneer club property. We tried to instil into the children the sense of a new future that was bright with possibilities. This was hard to do in the middle of the economic and social hardships brought on by the collapse of everything they'd known as normal.

The camp had a basic structure to it, a framework of security and order, and it began (as had all the camps I'd attended) with a flag raising. This is when you gather at the flagpole and sing the national anthem. The problem was that after we'd all gathered around the flagpole we realized that there wasn't a national anthem worth singing or a flag worth raising.

In a fit of nervous energy I asked my friend and translator Olga if the old anthem was really that bad... couldn't we sing it just for this morning? She assured me that that would be the worst possible thing we could do.

Why? Because it was simply a song of lies.

After that episode I had a heart to heart with Olga. I asked her how she could continue to function without being incredibly angry with her country. I mean, the government had lied to her and her fellow citizens. Their deceit was outright – and outrageous. They'd changed the history textbooks and the maps of the world and had used national anthems of sheer profanity. How did she cope with it all?

Olga looked at me, with some pity at my naivety, as though at nineteen she had the wisdom of the ages, and said, "Oh Danielle. Russia may have lied to her people – but her people chose to believe the lies."

You see, lies – especially the blatant ones – need to be believed to have true power.

Once I hosted a speaking tour with Victor Malarek, an investigative journalist from Canada who spent ten years trying to track down the details of the global sex trade.

His findings are staggering. He says that the horrible evil of trading women for sex is allowed to exist in the world because of a lie. It's a lie that is blatant and ridiculous and rooted in deep issues around gender inequality. It's the lie that suggests that it's completely normal for a man to buy a woman's body for sex.

Victor outlines all the reasons that men and societies (even governments) give to justify the behaviour which allows men to take women, mostly oppressed and vulnerable women who are economically and socially powerless, and rape them, because the men have money in their pocket and an urge in their pants. The myth that this is normal behaviour not only sustains economic and gender-based injustice in Western brothels and escort agencies, but fuels the sex tourism that makes up the majority of global human trafficking.

People suggest that prostitution is the oldest profession but Victor suggests otherwise. Prostitution is the world's oldest *oppression* against women.

It always has been.

Think about it.

Prostitution means treating another person like property – to use and abuse and throw aside when we're done.

Now, I visit brothels.

I visit brothels hidden in nice suburbs all around my city. They are full of women who have not met many other women who would just like to see their faces. They are full of oppressed, marginalized, and exploited women who get visited on a regular basis by men who want to see something other than their faces.

This is not what governments (by failing to bring in legislation) or advertisements tell you. They tell you that being a prostitute is fun and liberating – a great way to make a load of cash and feel sexually free! Apparently some women say they consider prostitution liberating: the trouble is, I haven't met any. Eighty-six per cent of women who are involved in prostitution around the world would do anything else – *anything* else – if they thought they could. Not a very liberating statistic.

I go to visit prostitutes because I want to know them as people. People with names, and a history, and families, and connections. People with dignity and respect. People who deserve intimacy and relationship. Their value isn't based on their place in society, or limited because of what I think of their culture or their belief system. They are valuable because of who they are.

One time I found myself in the dark back room of a bondage and discipline brothel, a place where dominatrix women make men suffer and perform sexual acts that no one in a decent relationship would consider, not even for a moment. I remember with dread the notice I read in the waiting area on my first visit: "This is a medium B&D establishment. If you require services that will bruise, mark, apply extreme pressure or cause scarring… you'll need to renegotiate the price…" I cringed as I thought about the reality of life in this place and what went on there every day of the week.

The women took their breaks in the back room, still in their outfits so they were ready to respond if a customer arrived. We gathered around the coffee table, while bondage videos played in the background, flickering in my peripheral vision. My eyes kept wandering up the main wall, examining the pentagram that had been painted front and centre on it. It felt like the enemy had marked his territory, yet for some reason, at this moment it was extremely fun to invade it – with joy and cupcakes, home-made and full of sugary blessing and goodness. The extreme difference in reality was worth breathing in… a tea break in hell. That's what it felt like.

The women I met in here were extraordinary. They put up an incredible front, tough as nails, it would seem. But if you hung out for more than a few minutes, you'd see the signs of weariness and the results of darkness in their lives.

One girl and I started to talk long and hard about her life situation. Her story could've come out of a textbook. A foster kid, whose birth mother was a prostitute, she ran away from home at fourteen and got into drug addiction. By the time I met her, she'd climbed her way up from street prostitute to dominatrix, the top of the prostitution ladder, and was trying hard to feel good about herself.

I asked if I could pray for her and she readily agreed, with tears in her eyes. It was when I grabbed her hand to pray that I saw the marks. Fresh, self-harming gouges that were evidence of the deep darkness which threatened to

41

overwhelm her and consume her very life. Once I'd seen the telling marks and prayed, our relationship changed. She needed more than a tea break. She needed a breakout. And so, between the two of us, in the home of darkness, but in the presence of God's light, we made a plan over tea and cupcakes that could break her out of that hell for good.

All over the world, women are suffering like this. We need to expose the lies that trap them.

One classic lie suggests that men are doing the prostituted women a favour by buying their services – as though they are helping them out of poverty by paying to heap yet more sexual abuse on them.

Another classic is that if you ban prostitution you make it more likely that "nice" girls will get raped. That's such a convoluted minefield that I don't even know where to begin to debunk it. All it does is fuel baseless fears about what a world where gender equality is possible might look like.

Whole societies have believed these lies. As a matter of fact, in our current culture, the sex industry has hijacked the name of "womens' rights". They heap argument upon argument to bolster the myth that violence and sexual abuse, which are the harsh realities at the heart of prostitution, are actually liberating. That's sick.

The writers of *Half the Sky* have looked at ways of exposing these myths:

What policy should we pursue to try to eliminate that slavery [of prostitution]? Originally, we sympathized with the view that prohibition won't work any better against prostitution today than it did against alcohol in America in the 1920s. Instead of trying fruitlessly to ban prostitution, we believed it would be preferable to legalize and regulate it. The pragmatic "harm reduction" model is preferred by many aid groups, because it allows health workers to pass out condoms and curb the spread of AIDS, and it permits access to brothels so that they can more easily be checked for the presence of underage girls.

Over time, we've changed our minds. That legalize-and-regulate model simply hasn't worked very well in countries where prostitution is often coerced. Partly that's because governance is often poor, so regulation is ineffective, and partly it's that the legal brothels tend to attract a parallel illegal business in young girls and enforced prostitution. In contrast, there's empirical evidence that crackdowns can succeed, when combined with social services such as job retraining and drug rehabilitation and that's the approach we've come to favour.[1]

One country in particular decided to look behind the façade: Sweden.

Sweden led a revolutionary campaign to look at the causal factors of the global sex trade and its connection to prostitution.

They decided that if they were going to deal with the root causes of sexual violence against women they'd have to start dishing out some truth. So, they took a long look at prostitution to find out who were the women that were engaged in it (mostly poor, marginalized, exploited) and what exactly they were doing (deeply distressing things that would never be allowed in a relationship with any shred of dignity). They considered the costs involved to the women themselves: overwhelmingly, death, deeply disturbing trends of drug addiction, self-harm, and post-traumatic stress disorder. And they looked at the costs to society: policing, rehabilitation, medical treatment – and the ever-increasing demand for more and more women.

They decided that if they were going to tell the whole truth they would have to do it boldly. So they called prostitution what it was: violence against women.

In a stunning and radical move, instead of criminalizing the women, they criminalized the men. Being a prostitute is no longer illegal in Sweden. Visiting one is. Instead of dealing with the supply they dealt with the demand.

The reason that women become prostitutes is that men believe a lie. Until that lie is exposed and you start dealing in truth, you'll never solve the problem.

When I asked Swedish reformer Gunilla Ekberg her secret to getting to the truth, exposing the lie and changing a nation's mind, she told me that one of the key ingredients of the campaign was the ability to imagine a different world. The ability to step outside the norm, and to picture a whole new truth.

It's not the first time that change has come about in this way.

Over a hundred years ago Catherine Booth, co-founder of The Salvation Army, stood up and spoke the Word of God with great power – and found that God approved. She shocked an indoctrinated public who believed that women didn't have the right to preach.

A hot preacher and a fiery advocate for justice, Catherine wrote a manifesto on the subject of women preachers that was to become a trumpet call for women the world over, advocating women's right to preach the gospel.

What the manifesto did, backed up by Catherine's living example, was expose a lie. A lie that people in the church had believed in, and lived by, for generations. The myth that women weren't able to preach, because they were somehow inferior in intellect and ability. Therefore they weren't useful to God and they weren't allowed to use their gifts in public.

This lie was, and is, believed by men because it feeds some sort of ego and affords them power. It is also believed by many women. These women have been told over and over, from pulpits, and by fathers, mothers, and brothers, that they exist to serve men. They've been told that equality isn't actual but virtual. That we are equal but different. And by different, they mean subservient.

This isn't a new strategy. The transatlantic slave trade

was able to muster up many slaves who were against their own emancipation! The civil war in America found a bunch of slaves who thought it was God's will for them to stay enslaved. In so many ways it's just easier to believe than to challenge the lie.

Today, many women actually believe that God created them to serve under male authority. They live their lives, limiting their gifts and potential, submitting all they do and are to the men they marry and the men who lead their churches.

I have spoken to dozens of women who are now coming to grips with the reality of what this lie has done in limiting their potential and stopping God's kingdom from flourishing. Many others are still trying to explain themselves to churches that refuse to make room for their leadership gifts.

The thing is, I don't want to spend my life – and another generation – trying to catch up with Catherine Booth. We are called to finish what she started. We should be building on her revelation with fresh and creative ideas about how to empower people to be what God has called them to be. We should be giving them systemic freedom to pursue their callings and fan into flame the gifts that are embedded within them.

Surely this idea is worth the struggle?

Ideas are powerful things. I believe it's a God-inspired idea that women really can change the world. It's what we're meant to do.

CHAPTER FOUR

Invisible

The West has its own gender problems. But discrimination in wealthy countries is often a matter of unequal pay or underfunded sports teams or unwanted touching from a boss. In contrast, in much of the world discrimination is lethal... the global statistics on the abuse of girls are numbing. It appears that more girls have been killed in the last fifty years, precisely because they were girls, than men were killed in all the battles of the twentieth century. More girls are killed in this routine "gendercide" in any one decade than people were slaughtered in all the genocides of the twentieth century.

Half the Sky[1]

47

Throughout the world women are the victims of systematic discrimination, oppression, and sexual abuse. In many parts of the world they are trapped at home, denied basic democratic and economic rights, forced to carry out unpaid domestic labour, and subject to oppression and violence by men. Women and children are the main victims of the global sex trade. They are also the most impoverished societal group and are at the bottom of the economic ladder. And, although women make up more than 50 per cent of the world's population, they own less than 1 per cent of its land.

Women often bear the double burden of paid work and domestic labour – a life of unending toil. Women workers are routinely paid less than men for doing the same job, and often they don't enjoy the same legal protections as are afforded to men in the workplace. In sweatshops around the world, women workers are frequently abused, denied maternity leave, and subjected to degrading treatment. Domestic workers, particularly migrant workers, often fall outside the scope of labour laws entirely.

In many countries, laws restrict women's access to financial independence, discriminating against them in matters of employment, property, and inheritance. In addition, economic policies often discriminate against women, depriving them of sustainable means of livelihood.

Amartya Sen, the Nobel Prize-winning economist, has developed a gauge of gender inequality that is a striking reminder of the high stakes involved.

"More than 100 million women are missing," he wrote, in an essay in the *New York Review of Books* in 1990. Sen noted that, in normal circumstances, women live longer than men, so there are more females than males in much of the world, even in the poorer regions. But, in many places, women and girls have such a profoundly unequal status, that it's as though they've vanished... The implication of this is that about 107 million females are effectively missing from the globe today.

They are missing because they are women. It's "gendercide", and it's wrong.

So what can we do?

Muhammad Yunus is the founder of the Grameen Bank, the largest microcredit bank in the world. He received the Nobel Peace Prize in 2006 and is an expert in how to break the cycle of poverty, hardship and oppression in the poorest places of the world. Much of his work is done with women, because when women are empowered, when they are treated as though they actually exist, they can – and do – find creative and practical ways of lifting themselves out of extreme poverty.

The Grameen Bank and other microfinance organizations use a system based on the voluntary formation of small groups of people who provide mutual, morally binding, group guarantees, instead of the collateral required by conventional banks. One or two group members receive a small loan. Depending on their repayment performance, other members can then take out a loan and the money is constantly recycled, to everyone's benefit.

Time after time, it's the women who get involved. It's the women who take up the loans and who work hard to repay them. And it's the women who use the money they earn to feed, clothe, and educate their families.

It's the day-to-day experience of many microfinance organizations that when women are empowered, the whole community benefits.

Women like Rajalakshmi, a mother of three from the island of Pulicat, two hours north of Chennai, India. She used a loan to start a small business selling rice and saris in her village, and has become the leader of a self-help group in her community. She says that it has changed her life. "Before, we had only the men's income, but now, with our own money, we can stand on our own two feet," she explains.

And women like Joy, who found herself alone, caring for six children, after her husband died from malaria. Instead of giving up in despair, she started a brick-making business. With a small loan of £100, and some savings, she was able to buy a small piece of land and employ eight people to make bricks. Since 2003, she has taken several further loans to enlarge her business. The profits have allowed her to send her children to school.

When women are given the opportunity to help themselves, they prove to be reliable borrowers and astute entrepreneurs. They are perfectly capable of raising their own standard of living, improving their homes, reducing their dependency on their husbands, and giving their children better food and better access to education.

Microfinance charity Five Talents has made observations that give some of the reasons why women make good loan clients. Women are less likely than men to drink their money away. They are able not only to set clear priorities, but also to appreciate the longer-term consequences of the choices that they make. Women know how to trust each other. They work well in groups that are based on friendship and common values. This is particularly important when groups of small-scale entrepreneurs with different skills – for instance a tomato seller, a pig farmer, the owner of a grocery store, and a hairdresser – are jointly responsible for repaying loans.

Muhammad Yunus mentions that one of the greatest obstacles to setting up new microfinance initiatives in small villages in remote areas of his native Bangladesh is that the Muslim village leaders believe that Grameen Bank is a Christian conspiracy.

Why would they think that?

Muhammad himself is a Muslim. But the fact that the Grameen Bank is suspected of being a Christian conspiracy is a deep compliment and, even better, a deep call to those of us who call ourselves "little Christs".

Because we are supposed to be like that.

We are invited by God to usher in a different way of

living. It's a way of living that champions empowerment and freedom. For everyone: rich and poor, slave and free, male and female.

Jesus led the way by example and by the declaration of a new way of being that created equality in all aspects of life. What a high and holy calling it is to bear the name of Jesus and walk out that kind of liberating reality in the world!

❈ ❈ ❈

Empowerment is about the longing for restoration – the longing for Eden, before brokenness entered the world.

Because, despite popular notions (which are mostly based on myth, not scripture), Eve was made equal to Adam. The Genesis account of creation is one of the strongest biblical arguments for gender equality.

The word used in Genesis 2:18 and 20 to describe Eve is *'ezer*, which means "someone who saves" or "tutor". It's mostly translated as "helper", which to a Western mindset seems to suggest a submissive type of situation. But the same word, *'ezer*, is used of God as "the God who saves".[2] In the language of the Old Testament, a "helper" is someone who rescues others in times of need. The word doesn't denote domesticity or subordination. It indicates competency and superior strength.

There's no hint of anything like a hierarchical order existing between men and women in the Genesis account.

In fact, the opposite is clearly taught. Both man and woman were made in God's image (Genesis 1:26–27) and they both participated in God-ordained ministries without any differentiation between their roles (Genesis 1:28). The relationship that God established between the man and the woman before the fall was one of "non-hierarchical complementarity". We were made to be equal.

Actually, this truth sounds a bit normal now. But when the Genesis story was written, it was a counter-cultural explosion, in the context of the other creation myths that were around at the time. The dominant ones were from Egypt and Babylonia. These creation myths emphasized two main points: one was that only the ruler was created in the image of God. This of course made everyone else subject to God's authority through the person of whoever happened to be the current ruler. We all know the extent of oppression born out of this philosophy through the various ruling Pharaohs – including the enslavement of the Jews. The second main theme of the other creation stories was that women were treated with contempt by the gods themselves. This is particularly evident in the Babylonian creation myth, the *Enuma Elish*, which tells of the beginning of the world being born out of violence, jealousy and domestic abuse.

> The council of the gods tests Marduk's powers by having him make a garment disappear and then reappear. After passing the test, the council enthrones Marduk as high king and commissions him to fight

Tiamat (his mother). With the authority and power of the council, Marduk assembles his weapons, the four winds as well as the seven winds of destruction. He rides in his chariot of clouds with the weapons of the storm to confront Tiamat. After entangling her in a net, Marduk unleashes the Evil Wind to inflate Tiamat. When she is incapacitated by the wind, Marduk kills her with an arrow through her heart and takes captive the other gods and monsters who were her allies. He also captured her husband Kingu. After smashing Tiamat's head with a club, Marduk divided her corpse, using half to create the earth and the other half to create the sky complete with bars to keep the chaotic waters from escaping. The tablet ends with Marduk establishing dwelling places for his allies.[3]

I remember hearing Steve Chalke explain the contrast between Babylon's story of beginning and the Genesis account at a Stop the Traffik[4] conference. It is indeed stunning.

Not only does Genesis provide the concept of a loving God who creates out of his own fullness, but it also lays the groundwork of value which is deeply embedded in all of humanity – including the basics of human rights, justice, and freedom for all. God made man and woman in his own image and declared that they were *good*.

The radical notion that all of humanity (both women and men) was made in God's image was remarkable at the time. It still is.

It affirms that no one person (not even a supreme leader) has any more value than another. This immediately undermines any idea of slavery, of racial or gender discrimination, of any abuse of power. And it exposes the moral bankruptcy of oppressing women, since women themselves have intrinsic worth, sanctioned by the God who made us. This image of God in us is what gives us true value, a value not based on price, gender, culture, background or the whim of another human being. It's the essential part of who we are.

The Genesis creation story established equality as the foundation of the entire history of God's people on the earth. This truth is the most liberating of all. Not just for that time and for those people, but for us as well.

This is how we started. This is God's design. This is how He wanted it to be. Equality. Dignity. Value. Those qualities help us understand a loving God who created out of fullness, not out of vengeance or jealousy or violence.

That kind of positive image is meant to be reflected in our relationships. But, as the Genesis story continues, those relationships unravel. Sin and Satan enter the scene and brokenness rather than equality begins to characterize relationships. The first indication of a hierarchical order between the man and the woman developed after sin entered the world (Genesis 3:16).

Clearly the subordination of women to men wasn't part of God's original design for humanity. It resulted from the violation of God's creation order.

When people chose selfishness over God's best plan for them, it broke the best of creation, then broke all other relationships. Beginning with brokenness between the genders, it quickly moved to hostility between brothers, then to tribal prejudice, then to slavery. It developed into an incredible story of subjugation and oppression, with this thread of divine longing woven throughout, beckoning the whole created order towards the hope of restoration.

In a letter to the church in Rome (Romans 12), Paul says that our minds can literally be transformed by renewing them in Jesus. Jesus certainly thought differently from anyone else, before or since. He was incredibly good at challenging the culture, by testing religious sensibilities and worldly notions of power and success. He turned every accepted idea upside down in order to establish a new world: a new way of doing things, a new way of being.

Our calling, according to Paul, is to worship God as non-conformists, as people who don't bend to the dominant culture. It's simply a matter of tuning in to a different song. The kind of song that you can't get out of your mind, and you start to hum even though sometimes you forget the words.

And, once your mind starts to be transformed, and you get the song into you, you can start to celebrate. That's what Paul – and Jesus – suggest. And how do we celebrate?

Well, by using our gifts.

It's true – read it for yourself right there in Romans 12. One of the great ways in which the church celebrates God's goodness is by the release and empowerment of his people. All of God's people. Women and men. Paul is practical enough to suggest that if your gift is leadership, you should lead. If your gift is service, you should serve. If your gift is… you get the picture.

The problem I have with the church's continued reluctance to empower women is that we (those of us who follow Jesus) should be the ones who model an alternative approach to leadership. We're the ones with the Bible and the witness of the Holy Spirit. We're the ones to whom God has revealed, time and time again, through scripture, reason, tradition, and experience, that His heart is for everyone to be released to exercise their gifts.

Why? Why does God care about women's empowerment?

So that His redemption plan will transform the whole world.

The world is ready: the world needs transformation.

And it's starting to happen. Kofi Annan, Secretary-General of the United Nations from 1997 to 2006, said that women are the solution to global poverty. *The* solution.

The world is beginning to grasp that there is no policy more effective in promoting development, health, and education than the empowerment of women and girls.

On International Women's Day in March 2010, Navanethem ("Navi") Pillay, United Nations' High Commissioner for Human Rights, delivered a speech in which she declared, "I have much to celebrate on International Women's Day. In my lifetime, I have seen unimaginable change, in my own country and around the world. I have seen the power of ordinary people who have stood up against the injustices they faced and who have triumphed against all odds."[5]

She went on to explain that, as a woman of colour, raised in poverty, her early experiences were of gender, race, and class discrimination. "But today," she said, "I am celebrating the power of women, the power to overcome the particular vulnerabilities resulting from these multiple forms of discrimination."

Navi believes that the global economic crisis is having a disproportionate impact on women, as women make up the majority of the poor and disenfranchised people of the world. They face the loss of their economic and social rights, as well as civil and political rights. The recognition of all these rights, to which women are entitled, is fundamental to their empowerment.

But, rather than despair, Navi sees hope:

Despite the enormity of violence and discrimination against women, today I am celebrating. I am celebrating the power of women whose spirit cannot be broken, who survive and even thrive. I am celebrating the vision of equality between women and men that is enshrined in the framework of international human rights law, and our collective efforts to move towards that vision and make it a reality for all women and men around the world. I am also celebrating the growing number of men who understand that sex equality benefits men and women both, and who work to end violence and discrimination against women…

I see girls around the world growing up with a different sense of themselves than I and most women of my generation were given. These girls are powerful – they say no to harmful practices such as early marriage, female genital mutilation, and sexual harassment. They want to go to school and get an education. They want to be lawyers, doctors, judges, members of parliament. They want to change the world they live in. I know they will, and I celebrate these girls on International Women's Day. They are our future.

CHAPTER FIVE

Ball and Chain

When I was leading the social justice wing of The Salvation Army in Australia, we ran a campaign highlighting violence against women, particularly domestic abuse. We partnered with other women's groups and NGOs and, because we operate domestic violence shelters in many countries around the world, we had a lot of information about the realities and costs to society of this kind of violence.

The month before the campaign started, I kept running into different women who'd had similar experiences to each other. At the doctor's office I met a woman from India, eight months pregnant, who was running away from a violent husband. She was told by her family that, because she'd decided to leave her husband, the shame she'd brought down on them was so great that she'd be burned alive if she returned to India. Thankfully, we were able to help her with some accommodation and we got her a limited stay visa so she didn't have to return to that situation.

It was easy for me to dismiss this case as a cultural issue that I didn't really understand – until I ran into another friend. She had emigrated from Asia with her husband and two sons. When they landed in Australia her husband became very violent towards her. As she was a Christian, and attended a great church, she naturally turned to the Christian community for help. But when she told the pastor what was happening, she was stunned by his reply: "You need to return home and learn to submit to your husband."

She didn't know what to do or where to go. Because the pastor suggested she should stay, she stayed. Not long after, there was another violent incident. Her husband nearly strangled her to death. My friend was left partly paralyzed and her unborn child suffered brain damage. I couldn't believe it... This wasn't happening far away, in a time or place where women lacked the right to vote, to work or to hold property. It was happening here and now, in the twenty-first century, among people with laws and rights and education... We are talking about Christian people, making a mockery out of scripture and out of God.

Again, I thought I could maybe explain it away by cultural differences. But then I met Stacy. Stacy is as modern and as Westernized as they come. Raised in a Christian home, she is educated, bright, funny, and pretty. She met a guy in Bible College and they fell in love. But after they were married, he suddenly became very possessive and violent towards her. She didn't know what to do. Again, because she was a Christian, she went to her leadership for help. They told her that her job was to learn to submit. That she should love her husband more like Jesus. That the best solution was for her to go back home and pray more...

Aaahhhhhhhhhh! That is the sound of me losing my mind. I cannot believe that this is happening now. It sounds like some novel from the Dark Ages. The whole thing drives me nuts.

By the end of the month, I could no longer declare domestic violence against women to be a cultural issue or a race problem. It's a human problem.

Let's be honest – it's a Church problem. With this sort of witness about what marriage looks like, and with this sort of ignorance and prejudice against women, how can any thinking person see that we believe in a God who loves equality and dignity and justice? We face a lot of judgment – not just from the wounded women and their families, but from God Himself.

❀ ❀ ❀

Feminism was born out of a culture that devalued women, that wouldn't allow them to vote, considered them intellectually inferior, and, as a result, limited their involvement in the world.

Catherine Booth once wrote a scathing letter to her senior pastor after he preached a sermon about the intellectual limitations of women. The letter – apart from being evidence of the sheer lunacy of the original sermon – shows that the notion that women couldn't reason as well as men was a common belief at the time.

Women faced a whole raft of restrictions. They weren't allowed to compete in marathons or long-distance running races because too much running was thought to interfere with their ability to get pregnant or give birth. Incredibly, this notion continued in North America until the 1970s, when one brave woman dressed as a man and ran anyway.

Young women were considered to be the property of their fathers; wives were the property of their husbands. Until fifty years ago, women in many countries had no recognized grounds for divorce, they weren't legally allowed to own property in their own name, and they didn't have the right to keep their own children.

First-wave feminism, in the nineteenth and early twentieth centuries, was primarily focused on a woman's right to vote. The suffrage movement was concerned to make women not only visible, but also able to participate in civic life for the first time.

It's hard for women born recently even to imagine a world where such incredible gender injustices were possible – let alone once being the norm.

Conservative Christian women were at the heart of this first wave of feminism. Many Quakers and revivalists instigated and supported the various political campaigns to give women the vote in both North America and the UK. In its early days, feminism was connected to the Church, and it was intimately tied up with the campaign to abolish the slave trade. Both campaigns focused on equality, dignity, and freedom. During this period in its history the Church's newfound spirituality was matched by an intense desire to change the world and challenge ungodly and unjust practices.

The revivalist preacher Charles Finney (1792–1875) was a huge supporter of the suffrage movement. At his campaign meetings, he used to call people to the front to accept salvation. After they had made this public demonstration of their conversion, he would take them to a separate room to have a longer conversation about the impact of salvation on their lives. Part of that conversation included showing the new converts two petitions. One was about the abolition of the slave trade. The other was about women's suffrage. People who refused to sign were often told that they needed to return to the meeting and find true salvation...

The connection between spiritual freedom and the realities of justice in the present world were part of the early feminist agenda.

The second wave of feminism, the Women's

65

Liberation Movement, began in the 1960s and continued into the 1970s. The focus of this phase was largely around overturning legal obstacles to equality, and included a wide range of issues such as property rights, attitudes to women, sexuality, the family, women in the workplace, and reproductive rights.

Some of the directions this second wave took were in contrast to biblical ideas of justice and equality. Sexual promiscuity and abortion in particular, which were high on the feminist agenda, contravened Christian views. One result of this divergence is that today, in some churches, being a feminist is considered a bad thing. I've been called a feminist with disdain more times than I care to remember.

The thing is, true biblical feminism is incredibly important. It's based on the fundamental principles of equality and dignity. Without feminism, gender injustice will continue to thrive and women still won't be able to contribute towards a better world.

Many good Christians, who, no doubt, would die for "the Truth", still refuse to consider this truth; that we were created equal. The Bible simply does not support the doctrine of authoritarian male headship and female subjugation. But many Christians cling to traditional ideas about womanhood, even though those ideas are blatantly unbiblical.

When the scriptural texts which appear to create strongholds of female subjugation are read in context, and with historical accuracy, it's clear that these interpretations are inaccurate and self-serving. It's also clear that their originally intended meanings agree with Jesus' teaching, in which men and women are regarded as equal in terms of substance and value, privilege and responsibility, function and authority. And, when accurately interpreted, these passages agree with the activity of the Spirit throughout the centuries.

Based on biblical evidence, it's abundantly clear that women stand before God equal in every respect with men.

Christians need not be afraid of this truth.

I find it hard to believe that, for many girls, the question of what they want to do with their life is often answered not based on their gifts, or even their desires, but based on what their spouse or boyfriend thinks or wants. I can't tell you the number of women I've met who get their value from who they date or marry. Women can make very poor choices because of the pressure our culture imposes on them to have a spouse and settle down.

Now, I'm married and have two children. All of this is a deep blessing to me. But when I was thinking about marriage, and the possibility of getting married, I made a checklist.

I really did.

I made a list because I was terrified that choosing marriage would mean that I'd have to stop using my gifts and skills fully for God's kingdom. I thought that being married meant that I would have to be willing to take a back seat and become a supportive presence and lose my ability and deny my giftedness.

Now, just think about that for a minute. No one taught me this explicitly. But somehow, the prevailing Christian culture modelled and suggested the idea strongly enough for me to believe it. As a young girl, just discovering my gifts and my calling, I believed that choosing marriage meant in all likelihood denying my full potential. That's really twisted.

Can you see what's happened? The beautiful picture of marriage, of love and mutual submission, where two people become better together than they are apart, has been turned into a travesty of control and oppression. One person – always the woman – has to become less in order for the system to work.

My checklist sounds funny now, but it really wasn't. It wasn't a shallow thing at all. It summed up the essential things I was looking for in a life partner; the things on which I wasn't willing to compromise. I made it to protect myself from tyranny and – even worse – from becoming invisible. Since I made it I've met enough women who've made poor choices out of desperation to know that more women should make checklists.

The Salvation Army founders Catherine and William Booth also recommended that young people considering marriage should make a list. In his book *Letters to Salvationists on Love, Marriage, & Home*, General Booth said that, since many of the young people coming to meetings were unmarried, it was important that they had right views about marriage and the steps that lead up to it. In the chapter "The Choice of a Partner", he advised: "all whom it may concern, that they should, by prayer and reflection, settle upon a definite idea of the sort of person likely to prove suitable for a life companion".

His first qualifications for a potential partner were that they should have:

1. A present day personal relationship with Jesus Christ.
2. A godly life, resulting from the power of the Holy Spirit within, alive and well and active.
3. A heart controlled by the love of God and people.

Catherine Booth gave her own advice to women seeking a life partner through marriage – and suggested that her husband's views of women and their role should be on the list of requirements!

Every woman needs a checklist. Shared egalitarian views should be at the top. Because, even today, Western ideas about marriage are often based on inequality.

Think about it. For one thing, the "giving away" part of a wedding ceremony is based on the tradition of women being the property of men.

One young couple decided to do things differently because they wanted an egalitarian wedding ceremony. Anna, the bride, explains:

> We decided to replace the "giving away" ceremony after discovering that it originated during a time

when daughters were considered to be the property of their father. The father's giving away of his daughter signified the transfer of his ownership of her to her new husband, who assumed authority over her.

When I reached the front of the church on my wedding day, instead of giving me away, my parents simply hugged me and sat down. Their presence in this way signified their blessing over our marriage, while still making it clear that we did not believe that a transfer of ownership was taking place. I willingly chose to enter into marriage as an adult and an individual. I was no one's property.[1]

When I was in the planning stages of getting married I ran into a roadblock. I had to change my name. There was something about the idea that unnerved me. I'm not even sure why. But I started to wonder why women changed their names. The only answer I could come up with was that it was cultural. Lots of people suggested that it was biblical, and one woman told me it was "against church policy" for women to keep their maiden name. I couldn't find anything like that anywhere in the Bible. Actually, the only text I could find in relation to this, that a man will leave his house to cling to his wife (Genesis 2:24), rather suggests an opposite idea.

So I asked the man I was planning to marry, "Would you take my name?" He thought and prayed about it, because he's very godly and secure – he isn't threatened by asking questions to get to deep truths. But in the end he didn't see the value in it.

That's when it hit me. If there was no value in him changing his name to "seal his love" for me, then where was the value in me doing the same? Is it really love that demands that another person should do something that they wouldn't do themselves? Or is it something rather more controlling?

So, I decided to keep the name that my husband fell in love with. To stay the person I was, and to believe and strive to be even better, because I was married. More fully myself, not less. And that's what marriage was always intended to be about.

I was on an immersion mission in Zambia a few years ago, during which I had the privilege of going on visits to the remote villages that surrounded the town where we were based. I went with a group of young people from the mission I was working with and they were very enthusiastic about evangelism. Because I was a special visitor they had arranged for me to visit the headman of each village.

One of my Zambian colleagues told me about his own father, who was the head of his village. This man had ten wives and my friend was the first son of his first wife. The conversation quickly turned to the realities of, and questions about, polygamy. Was it wrong?

The group I was talking with suggested that polygamy only goes wrong if the headman is a bad man.

"If the headman is good", said my Zambian friend, "then the situation can be fine."

I thought about this for a while and finally agreed. Everyone looked surprised. I explained that, if I was really honest, I could use a lot of extra help around my house and with my children. So I'd decided that I could use an extra husband.

They immediately started to protest. "No, that's impossible! It wouldn't be right to have more than one husband," they responded – with some heat.

"I don't understand," I told them. "Why can't the arrangement work both ways? If it's a purely pragmatic way of arranging things, then surely it could work either way round?"

Their reaction to my suggestion is an indication that polygamy as a system is fundamentally biased against women. It's another example of a structure that only works if women are subjugated and submissive. As soon as the situation is reversed it's a completely different story.

❈ ❈ ❈

Now, many people say they have a very high view of women and yet they are still in error about the roles women play in the church and in the world. Men continue to believe that women are distinct from men in that they differ in their giftings and that it was God's design to relegate women to a submissive role to support men as the men lead the world.

N. T. Wright makes a good point that is worth

mentioning here. He suggests that it's clearly an error to declare there are no differences between men and women. It's obvious that biological differences exist. And much work has been done on possible emotional and spiritual differences between the genders. The real point is not that there is no difference, but that there is no equality distinction, and there are no limitations in using our gifts in and for God's kingdom.[2]

This is important. N. T. Wright suggests that there is a danger in saying that men and women are exactly the same. If we ignore the reality of our bodies, and the fact that we were created male and female, we risk falling into a similar trap to the Gnostics in the first centuries after Jesus. They were a group of people who tried to suggest that this world – which includes our bodies and anything physically rooted here – doesn't matter. The result of this teaching is the belief that there's a higher spiritual plane we can live on, blithely ignoring the realities of everyday life.

We don't want to deny our gender. We just don't want to be defined or limited by it. What I'm suggesting is not that women and men are the same, but that the gifts of the Spirit are – and they are given to both men and women in equal measure and are given for the expansion of God's kingdom. Yet even today some preachers suggest that women are valuable only for some things and in some ways and for some work.

This is a lie.

It's swallowed hook, line, and sinker by many churches – indeed whole denominations – because it's easier to believe than the truth. Co-stewardship is at the heart of God's design for humanity.

It's clear from reading the Genesis account of creation that God created humanity – men and women – as a reflection of His own character, which is community. God Himself is three persons: Father, Son, and Spirit. Even before He created the world, God the Trinity was a relational being.

And yet, we challenge this idea of loving, active interrelationship, where distinct and different persons work equally towards the same goal, because we want to believe the lie that it's a man's right to lead and a women's purpose is to follow. But what if a woman has the gift of leadership? My Bible suggests that she should lead. God the Father agrees. So do the teachings of Jesus. And so does the witness of the Holy Spirit.

Separate from the phases of feminism, the Church has, as a movement, developed its own views on women and their position in the world. Broadly speaking, there are three main theories.

1. *Patriarchy*. This view holds to exclusively male leadership in the home, in the church, and in public life. Women are regarded as submissive helpers, childbearers, and homemakers, and are discouraged from having careers outside the home. The rationale for this view comes from a scriptural interpretation

that maintains that God is exclusively male and that distinct gender roles are part of the creation order.

This is the old-fashioned, nuts view. Women are viewed as property and their husbands are expected to speak for them. It's apparently OK for men to subjugate, dominate, and generally demean women.

2. *Complementarian*. This position is similar to the patriarchal view of men and women. It holds that men and women, although "equal in personhood", were created to exercise different but complementary roles and responsibilities in marriage, the family, the church, and society. The main tenets of this view were reviewed in the *Danvers Statement on Biblical Manhood and Womanhood* in 1987.

The problem with the complementarian view is that defining roles based on gender turns out to be much like defining roles based on ethnicity, or age... Functional distinctions based on gender difference always seem to trump the idea of spiritual equality. Adherents of the complementarian view assign leadership roles to men and support roles to women. Women cannot exercise ministry – or are restricted to certain types of ministry – in the church. They are allowed limited participation in decision-making processes, but the ultimate authority in marriage and in the Church rests firmly with the men. When push comes to shove, the man is the boss, and the woman submits.

3. *Egalitarianism* holds that all human persons are created equal in God's sight. Men and women are of equal fundamental worth and moral status. Both have fully equal authority and responsibility in marriage, in society and in ministry. Both men and women are free to use their gifts and obey their calling, to the glory of God. A key text is the previously mentioned Galatians 3:28 (see *Chapter One*).

This view is applied not only to gender, but also to religion, skin colour, age and any other difference between individuals. It does not imply that we are clones, all having the same skills, abilities, interests, physiological, intellectual, or genetic traits. It is based on a correct interpretation of scripture.

In my view, feminism in this century has been hijacked by economics – an amoral agenda that has led to the oppression, with renewed vigour, of more women in the name of "freedom" than ever before.

Christian responses to this oppression are often reactionary. They come from men who are reacting out of fear to what they perceive to be new cultural challenges to their own authority, power and position. The Church is simply part of a dominant culture that continues to exploit, subjugate, and humiliate women.

I regularly have conversations with people in the Church who are confused about the position of women and their equality in both value and in role. I have conversations with women and with men both young and old from a variety of denominations who simply don't understand that there is a good solid biblical framework for equality. The reality of this is tragic, because it means that, far from being a change agent in the world, the Church is busy fighting itself over what its position is on the issue of women. Rather than being salt and light and championing equality and dignity, it's stuck in the Dark Ages and is a stench in the nostrils of an empowering God.

Some days, I'm tired of having this conversation.

I'm exhausted because of all the women I know who are sidelined in their ministry and limited in their potential by small-minded, male-driven agendas of control and domination.

I'm worn out because of all the women I know who are incredibly gifted and yet struggle with their call to leadership, or their giftedness, not because of some sort of innate problem with their self-esteem, but because of a cultural norm that continues to communicate a lie – that their potential is limited by their gender.

I've got a restoration longing deep within my bones, because I've been infected by a holy calling, demonstrated through empowering every day as I use God's given gifts for his glory.

I've got a longing that defies the culture – that chooses a different way to live.

I've got a hunger for a different value system, a way of life that has at its core freedom and empowerment for everyone – women included.

I want to look behind the burqa, through the brothel, and past the poverty to see into the eyes of women, created with dignity, who deserve respect and equal freedoms.

Part Two

What the Bible Says

CHAPTER SIX

The Whole Truth and Nothing But

OK. So this is where we get to look in some detail at what the Bible says about women. There are whole books dedicated to this subject and I don't want to rehash the same ground. I do, however, want to debunk the lies that rely on mishandling scripture in order to keep women oppressed.

Katharine Bushnell was a remarkable missionary, reformer, and evangelist who died in 1946. As well as a groundbreaking book, *God's Word to Women*, she wrote a pamphlet, *Covet to Prophesy*, in which she suggested that:

> The clearing away of misconception and misinterpretation is demanded in order to remove impediments that block the progress of the Church.

> The question is much more than a woman question. It concerns the Church preparing the way for a more complete fulfillment of God's will as to a general outpouring of His Spirit upon believers – a fulfillment in completeness of what we saw in part in the Welsh Revival, even the pouring out of His Spirit upon "all flesh," without regard to caste, class or sex, foretold by Joel the prophet and realized on the Day of Pentecost.[1]

This is why the empowerment of women is so important. The final fulfilment of God's plan for the whole of humanity is at stake.

I think it's important to recognize that, despite scriptural authority and solid biblical exegesis, some people still continue to believe that God has some sort of deliberate plan that subjugates women and limits their involvement in his kingdom. Proponents of this idea disguise their true agenda behind a call to spiritual truth. Provided that the "truth" is interpreted their way.

In fact, despite the deep and liberating truths of God's plan for women, some passages of scripture are frequently misused to justify the oppression of women. Dennis Preato writes:

> It is a travesty that men have systematically denied women the opportunity to utilize the full extent of their gifts for God's glory. This denial is based on a few highly problematic passages in Scripture, such as 1 Corinthians 14:34–35 and 1 Timothy 2:12.

Perhaps the obvious must again be stated: sound hermeneutical principles warn against drawing unwarranted inferences from passages fraught with numerous interpretive issues. Yet, despite this knowledge, scholars, church leaders, and lay people continue to utilize such passages to deny or limit women the full exercise of their God-given gifts.[2]

On the other hand, there is a huge group of Christians trying to speak the truth in love and justice. They are attempting to understand what the Bible really says, delving deep into its context to find out its true meaning and how that meaning applies today. Their findings, as Dr Gilbert Bilezikian reports, show that,

The organization of the Christian community is never described as a gender-based hierarchy in the Scriptures. To the contrary, it is the doctrine of the community of oneness that sets the norm (Matthew 19:4–6; John 17:11, 20–23; Acts 4:32; Romans 12:4–5; 1 Corinthians 12:12–14; Ephesians 4:4–6). The practical implementation of this oneness is summarized in Galatians 3:28: racial distinctions (Jew/Greek), class distinctions (slave/free), and the gender distinction (male/female) are declared to have become irrelevant to the functioning of Christian communities. The compelling mandate for this radical restructuring of community is given as: "for you are all one in Christ".[3]

This isn't a small group of women who have liberal

tendencies and "hate men" because they "can't get one themselves". This is a group of dedicated Christians, men and women, from different faith traditions and denominations who, through the study of scripture, the application of reason, and the experience and witness of the Holy Spirit, have come to the conclusion that it's God's will that women be treated with dignity and respect and be empowered to use their gifts for God's kingdom on earth.

The solid foundation of sound and helpful biblical exegesis has been around for a long time but it still hasn't changed the minds of those who would keep women subservient, unfulfilled, and oppressed. So the true answer has to be more than just knowledge. It must be a deep revelation within our spirits, and a real willingness on the part of both women and men to submit to God's authority together.

To really get at the liberating truth we need to not only know the Bible, but also know why it matters and how to apply what it says. We discover truth through the fourfold grid of scripture, reason, tradition, and experience. We need to know more than what the Bible says. We need to know what it *means*. And we get at its meaning through understanding its context. Only then will we be able successfully to challenge the cultural norms that constrain and limit us. The deep injustices and harmful prejudices that are based on nothing more biblical than a skewed belief that gender-based roles are what define us.

And, at the risk of sounding too pragmatic, is it really possible for the Church to achieve its objective of fulfilling Jesus' command to go into the whole world and preach the gospel while over 50 per cent of its members are tied up and restricted in their ability to fight the enemy and lead the charge? Just because they are women?

Dr Bilezikian puts it like this: "What is at stake is not the role of women as much as the definition of the church as authentic biblical community. Is it possible for a local church to aspire to define itself as biblical community when more than half its constituency is excluded from participating in the most significant aspects of its life?"

The damage that is done to the image of God in the world through Church doctrine that is prejudiced against women is hard to estimate.

What is particularly difficult for me in all of this is that Jesus put a premium on the fact that the world would recognize the disciples because of the way they treated each other – with love. The kind of love that respected every individual. The kind of love that knew no Greek or Jew, or slave or free, or male or female. The kind of love that was a deliberate attack on the prevalent culture, which insisted that a person's value was based on usefulness, position, and cultural norms.

Paul the apostle goes to incredible lengths to demonstrate that the gospel doesn't put up barriers between people. It doesn't reinforce gender-based injustices. It doesn't accept gender bias. Actually, it destroys prejudice, oppression and the lies that seek to keep us apart from each other. When Paul sent back a slave to Philemon he sent him not as a slave but as a brother in Christ. What happens when a slave becomes a brother? He is no longer a slave. Jesus' early followers didn't need to start a petition against slavery – the practice simply dissolved, through the new way that people started treating each other. With equality, dignity, and respect. With values based on the witness of God's Holy Spirit within them.

The gospel of Jesus is so revolutionary that it challenges the culture from the inside out. And Jesus knew that people would want to be part of that radical new community.

What happens when we contrast this with the view that insists that God is gender biased and prejudiced against women because of some sort of hierarchical urge on His part? If you try and explain some of the key truths of the Bible in hierarchical terms, you'll find it can't be done. Take the doctrine of the Trinity, for instance. The Trinity is a mystery of mutual love and submission that can't be fully explained or understood. All three persons of the Godhead relate to one another in equal love and trust. Marriage is supposed to represent that mystery – and yet, as we've seen, many people in the Church insist on making marriage a transaction of power and authority. Women continue to be told that they must submit to ungodly leadership in the Church and in the home, making a mockery out of God's plan for the world.

This kind of thing has got to stop. It doesn't just limit women. It limits the gospel.

Dennis Preato explains that, "Scripture teaches us that the gifts and callings of God are given to all members of the body of Christ by the Holy Spirit (Romans 12:3–8; 1 Corinthians 12:4–11; Ephesians 4:7–11; 1 Peter 4:10–11). None of these gifts or offices is the exclusive prerogative of men. I believe this oppressive behavior against women grieves the Holy Spirit and hinders the Spirit's work in the Church. Much confusion in the church today over 'women in ministry' results from Bible scholars and others who fail to rightly divide and present God's truth."

We can't keep on like this. There are still cultures in the world today that treat women as badly as they were treated when Jesus walked among us on earth, and some are even worse. Jesus' response was to live in a different way, empowering women and challenging and changing societal norms. His example is a clear indication that the empowerment of women is of the utmost importance to the advancement of God's kingdom upon earth and the expression of God's justice. Because God doesn't use women as a default position when He can't find any good men to do the job. It's something He has always planned to do, from the beginning. Women are meant to co-steward the earth. Women are meant to bring about God's kingdom. Women who are released into their callings are a major part of God's plan for the world.

CHAPTER SEVEN

Words Have Power

The actual translation of many of the problematic passages regarding the status of women in the Bible and in the Church is an important issue. I think many times we forget that the translation of the scriptures from the languages in which they were originally written is not a perfect process.

As a matter of fact, all the major translations have tried to keep updating their research and their strategies around effective use of the English language in order to best represent what the writers of the Bible actually meant. Consider this story by Don Richardson, published in *Decision* magazine, April 2010:

> In the early 1600s, when King James commissioned an authorized translation of the Bible in English, the translators faced a conundrum. Paul, in 1 Timothy

1:10, lists slave traders among those whom God's law reproves. Dare they translate it correctly, knowing that many nobles – including perhaps King James himself – were engaged in slave trading or benefiting from its profits?

Would an honest rendering of the Greek term "andrapodistes" cost the translators their freedom? Or their heads? For whatever reason – fear, bias, pressure from the king himself – that one important Greek word ended up innocuously under-translated as "menstealers", that is, kidnappers. Ironically, millions of Christians, who were utterly disdainful of kidnapping, continued tolerating the most egregious form of kidnapping – slave trading – for another 200 years.

Think of it! If 1 Timothy 1:10 had been translated correctly as "slave traders" in the early 1600s, surely abolitionists like William Wilberforce would have arisen in western civilization a century or two earlier. Slavery might have been abolished before the American colonies formed, in which case there would have been no need for 600,000 Americans to perish in the civil war that belatedly banned it. Alas!

This miscommunication of the Gospel highlights how important it is for believers to proclaim the whole truth of Scripture clearly and faithfully. For only in God's pure Gospel is the power of salvation revealed.[1]

The issue of accurate translation is huge – particularly when it comes to women. Words have power.

A similar dumbing down has happened in Psalm 68:11. The correct translation is given in the New American Standard Bible: "The Lord gives the command; The women who proclaim the good tidings are a great host."

But other translations leave the women out. The New International Version has: "The Lord announced the word, and great was the company of those who proclaimed it." The Authorized King James Version has: "The Lord gave the word: great was the company of those that published it." And the New Living Translation chooses: "The Lord gives the word, and a great army brings the good news."

This is an end-times prophecy, in which an army of women evangelists is going to lead the battle. But some versions of the Bible omit the women altogether. And many churches omit the women, too.

❈ ❈ ❈

I was at a pastor's conference in Dallas, Texas when I heard a talk by Ed Silvoso. He has a theory that the enemy – Satan – has been strategically attacking women since the beginning. He cited Genesis 3:15: "And I will put enmity between you and the woman, and between your offspring and hers; he will crush your head, and you will strike his heel." The victorious conclusion to this enmity is revealed in Romans 16:20: "The God of peace will soon crush Satan under your feet", where Paul is referring to the Church.

As Silvoso slowly and graciously broke open the scriptures to reveal Satan's attack on women and God's real, perfect plan for us, the whole place became alive with revelation. If you could hear the sound of pennies dropping in people's minds and hearts, the noise would've been deafening.

At the end of the talk, Silvoso asked any woman who had been harmed or oppressed to stand up.

Almost every woman stood.

Tragically, this is the reality for many women, not just in the world, but also women in the Church, today.

Then he asked all the men who wanted to follow God's plan of redemption and fullness, rather than the enemy's plan of destruction and brokenness, to find a woman who was standing up, kneel before her and ask for her forgiveness.

The place was awash with sobbing. Men were sobbing as the realization of the dreadful cost involved in oppressing women dawned on them. Women were sobbing because of the realities of their own hurt and brokenness and the wonderful witness of what God can do through divine revelation and obedient, humbled hearts.

When I was leaving the building after the session had wrapped up, I met a father who had brought his estranged daughter with him that night. She had left the Church many years previously and was embittered against the Lord. That night she had turned to her father with tears streaming down her face and said, "If this is Christianity, count me in."

I agree with the theory that it was God's original design to empower women to defeat the enemy. And Satan mounted a specific counter-attack. It makes sense. What other explanation could there be for the seemingly systemic and consistent assaults against women around the globe?

This makes it even more essential that we figure out how best to advance God's kingdom come and start living this liberation in the day to day.

❈ ❈ ❈

When we read the Bible and try and work out what it means, we must keep in mind who its writers were, who its first audience was, and why it was written. Some fundamentalists suggest that the minute we do this we are twisting the Bible for our own purposes. The opposite is true. Context is the key to any conversation about the Bible and what it means.

One commentator tells the story of how, when he was a boy, he misbehaved and was noisy in church, so his mother told him to be quiet. She shushed him because he was speaking out loud in church. How ludicrous it would be if, twenty-five years later, and with a couple of degrees in theology, he was asked to preach but felt he had to decline because his mother had once told him not to speak out loud in church!

But this is exactly the sort of false logic that has been applied to some key Bible passages. They've been taken completely out of context and been misinterpreted to "prove" that women shouldn't speak in church.

We must take context seriously.

N. T. Wright spoke about context in a lecture he gave on women and leadership in the Church. When we read any Bible text, he says, we must be careful about discerning the writer's intention. Was the passage we are reading intended to build up God's Church, "men and women, women and men alike"? The Bible writers such as Paul were concerned to apply their teaching in their own particular context and the circumstances of the early Church, to whom they were writing. Wright concludes: "So we must think and pray carefully about where our own cultures, prejudices and angers are taking us, and make sure we conform, not to any of the different stereotypes the world offers, but to the healing, liberating, humanizing message of the gospel of Jesus."[2]

In 1971 Leonard Swidler wrote a fantastic article for *The Catholic World* magazine, entitled "Jesus was a Feminist". I know this because I wanted to call this book by that title. Considering the year in which he published his article, which is still an important resource, it's a sad reminder that the Church has wasted a lot of time on this issue. Swidler has extended his research since 1971 and has now published his own book with the same name. "Jesus was a Feminist" highlights the importance of understanding context as a tool for arriving at a true understanding of the expressed attitude of Jesus towards women.

The way in which women were treated in the Palestine of Jesus' day was extremely oppressive. Their condition was bleak. Once we understand this, we can see how revolutionary Jesus' actions towards and reactions to women really were. Every encounter Jesus had with a woman in each of the four Gospels was incredibly counter-cultural. Almost unbelievably so. Context is key to how we understand this truth.

Swidler put it like this:

The status of women in Palestine during the time of Jesus was very decidedly that of inferiors… women were not allowed to study the Scriptures (Torah). One first-century rabbi, Eliezer, put the point sharply: "Rather should the words of the Torah be burned than entrusted to a woman…"

In the vitally religious area of prayer, women were so little thought of as not to be given obligations of the same seriousness as men. For example, women, along with children and slaves, were not obliged to recite the Shema, the morning prayer, nor prayers at meals. In fact, the Talmud states: "Let a curse come upon the man who must needs have his wife or children say grace for him…"

> Moreover, in the daily prayers of Jews there was a threefold thanksgiving: "Praised be God that he has not created me a gentile; praised be God that he has not created me a woman; praised be God that he has not created me an ignorant man."[3]

Swindler is showing us how the culture of Jesus' time treated and thought about women in the days when Jesus walked and taught in and around Palestine. The reality, of course, is that these incredibly prejudicial and hate-filled prayers aren't biblical. But they are an important example of how prejudice distorts reality. If you repeat something often enough it starts to colour your thinking. And, soon enough, what you think becomes the reason for what you do. How we view things eventually turns into actions that have deep ramifications. That's why it's imperative that we offer correction to what some people suggest are "biblical" views on women when they are really just the entrenched views of their own prejudicial culture.

Swidler continues: "Rabbinic sayings about women also provide an insight into the attitude toward women: 'It is well for those whose children are male, but ill for those whose children are female… At the birth of a boy all are joyful, but at the birth of a girl all are sad…When a boy comes into the world, peace comes into the world; when a girl comes, nothing comes… Even the most virtuous of women is a witch… Our teachers have said: 'Four qualities are evident in women: They are greedy at their food, eager to gossip, lazy and jealous.'"

❂ ❂ ❂

Context sheds light on the scripture most often used to disqualify women from leadership in the church, 1 Timothy 2:11–15. Dr Bilezikian points out that the same passage of scripture places equally restrictive requirements upon men regarding leadership and ministry. A man's credentials for leadership rest upon his family status (1 Timothy 3:4 – 5:12). The letter to Timothy is unambiguous. If a man aspires to church leadership – teaching, having oversight of church administration – then it is essential that he should be married (to just one wife!) and that his children should be submissive. He must manage his own household well – "for if someone does not know how to manage his own household, how will he care for God's church?" (1 Timothy 3:5).

Dr Bilezikian observes that such stipulations disqualify not only women, but also single men; men who are married, but childless; men who only have one child; men whose children do not believe; men whose children are too young to make their own profession of faith; men whose children are, despite faith and a submissive attitude, insufficiently respectful. Very few church leaders would be left!

These remarkably strict and unyielding requirements are all the more amazing, as Dr Bilezikian notes, because other New Testament passages (Matthew 19:11–12, 1 Corinthians 7:25–35) endorse the idea of singleness for those in leadership roles. A further complication is that throughout the New Testament it is made clear that spiritual gifts for Christian ministry are bestowed quite without regard to marital or social status – or, for that matter, gender!

Of course, a few moments' reflection on the Scriptures will throw light upon these apparent contradictions. The churches which feature in the letters to Titus and Timothy are far from healthy, and the measures Paul proposes are of a remedial nature. In fellowships in crisis, what is needed is leadership from mature, proven managers. The same is equally true today. This does not undermine the general New Testament pattern of full participation by the whole constituency of a healthy church.[4]

Often it's all too easy to take a verse or two of scripture and apply them in ways that are inconsistent with the rest of scriptural witness. It's really important when we're determining what the Bible says and why it matters that we listen to the whole counsel of scripture. This will help us with context and application. Much of the teaching around women being inferior to men is centred on a verse or two of scripture that is misunderstood and interpreted so that it's out of place with the rest of the witness of scripture.

Those who suggest that women shouldn't lead in the church have a hard time understanding why God set Deborah apart as a leader, hero and judge in Israel. Sometimes this is explained away as being pre-Jesus – as though God, who is the same yesterday, today, and forever, got it wrong in the Old Testament. Another suggestion appears to imply that things simply got worse in the New Testament and God decided to really clamp down on women! This of course is ludicrous when you think about it.

Then there's Junia, a chief apostle in the New Testament and clearly a woman. We'll have a closer look at her later.

The point I want to make here is simply that, in order to be consistent, those who argue against women leading in the Church have to either reduce scripture to mean something else, or believe that God used Deborah and Junia in spite of His own plan for women. Or they maintain that Junia must have been a man, despite the obvious nature of her gender, or they have to make up some other nonsense. The reality is that, seen in the light of God's design throughout the whole of the Bible, women have always had a radical role in planting and establishing His kingdom.

Obviously we don't have time to look through the whole Bible, but what we can do is take some scriptural themes and apply them to our lives. This is a valid exegetical exercise. It's important to do it.

CHAPTER EIGHT

Jesus the Feminist

Jesus called himself the "Son of Man". The Greek word for this is *anthropos*, which means "humankind" – that is, both male and female. Even the title that He gave himself showed Jesus' inclusive attitude towards women.

In fact, Jesus vigorously promoted the dignity and equality of women in the midst of a very male-dominated society. This is an amazing thing in itself. Considering that most, if not all, of the rabbis, plus the Pharisees, the Romans, the laws and the customs, were all united in their horrible treatment of women – Jesus really stands out. In every interaction Jesus had with women He showed respect towards them and treated them as equal human beings. His whole attitude was an incredible contrast to the cultural norms of His day.

And this must have been deliberate, a choice that Jesus

made. Because He knew that it was important. Leonard Swidler points out that, "The fact that the overwhelmingly negative attitude toward women in Palestine did not come through the primitive Christian communal lens by itself underscores the clearly great religious importance Jesus attached to his positive attitude – his feminist attitude – toward women: feminism, that is, personalism extended to women, is a constitutive part of the Gospel, the Good News, of Jesus."[1]

Jesus continually broke with the traditions, religious law, and attitudes of the time regarding women. He continually affirmed women, honouring them, encouraging them in their faith, giving them dignity, equality, and value, and talking about them to men as positive examples of faith.

Jesus showed compassion for women's needs, even risking the hostility of the religious leaders on numerous occasions to receive ministry from women and to minister to them himself. Every time He spoke with a prostitute, every time He touched a dead person and every time He received things from "dirty" people – which included women – He offended the religious laws of His day. The strict standards of ritual cleanliness were only increased when it came to religious teachers, like Jesus himself. So when the woman broke perfume over His feet and washed them with her hair, or the woman with the issue of blood touched His robe, or He took the hand of the dead daughter of Jairus, or when Mary sat at His feet listening to His teaching – whenever those occasions happened, they defied all the normal rules of that society. Jesus' actions upturned the traditional expectations around rabbi/student relationships and totally offended the gender-biased laws of that time. Laws which limited and disallowed women.

The Gospels not only reveal Jesus' unique attitude towards women and distinctive relationship with them, but also show the emerging pattern of God's release of women into liberty and into ministry. Jesus encouraged women to be disciples, allowing them to travel with Him as companions. He revealed truths about himself to women, often before He revealed these same truths to the men.

Commentator Dee Alei says that "Jesus' words and actions leave no doubt as to His position regarding women. He laid a sure foundation during the three years of His ministry on the earth for their release as valued witnesses, teachers and leaders in the emerging Christian Church."[2]

Jesus and women disciples

A number of women, married and unmarried, were regular followers of Jesus.

In Luke 8:1–3, several are mentioned by name in the same sentence as the twelve disciples: "He made his way through towns and villages preaching and proclaiming the Good News of the kingdom of God. With him went the Twelve, as well as certain women… Mary… Joanna… Susanna; and many others… who provided for them out of their resources" [NJB]. Mark 15:40–41 refers to three women: Mary Magdalene, Mary the mother of James, and Salome, who had followed Jesus in Galilee and ministered to Him, caring for His needs. The Greek word translated in Luke as "provided for" and in Mark as "ministered to" is *diekonoun*, the same basic word as "deacon". In the early church, deacons carried out the same sort of tasks as these women undertook in ministering to Jesus.

In a culture where men were encouraged to thank God that they had not been born a woman, the fact that Jesus welcomed women into His inner circle is revolutionary. He didn't hold women at arm's length. He allowed them to get close to Him.

"The significance of this phenomenon of women following Jesus about, learning from and ministering to Him, can be properly appreciated when it is recalled that not only were women not to read or study the Scriptures, but in the more observant (traditional) settings they were not even to leave their household, whether as a daughter, a sole wife, or a member of a harem", says Leonard Swidler.[3]

Jesus and women thinkers

Jesus clearly did not think of women's roles in culturally restricted terms. He quite directly rejected the stereotype that a woman's place is in the home.

During His visit to the house of Martha and Mary (Luke 10:38–42), Martha took the typical woman's role: "Martha was distracted with much serving" [ESV]. Mary however, took the supposedly male role; she "sat at the Lord's feet and listened to his teaching" [ESV]. Martha apparently thought that Mary was out of place in choosing to do this, for she complained to Jesus.

Jesus' response was a refusal to force all women into the stereotype. He treated Mary first of all as a person, who was allowed to set her own priorities, and in this instance had "chosen the better thing". She had used her own autonomy, her intellect and spirit, to make a rational choice to distance herself from the frantic domestic activity that was going on. And Jesus applauded her decision: "It will never be taken from her" (NCV).

"It is difficult to imagine how Jesus could possibly have been clearer in his insistence that women were called to the intellectual, the spiritual life, just as were men," says Leonard Swidler.[4] Set against the cultural ban on women engaging in intellectual pursuits or acquiring any religious authority by studying the scriptures or studying with the rabbis, Jesus is once again revealed as a revolutionary.

N. T. Wright makes this point about the story of

Martha and Mary: "Devotion is undoubtedly part of the importance of the story, but far more obvious to any first-century reader, and to many readers in Turkey, the Middle East and many other parts of the world to this day, would be the fact that Mary was sitting at Jesus' feet within the male part of the house rather than being kept in the back rooms with the other women."[5]

Mary is "sitting at his feet"; a phrase that doesn't mean what it would mean today – the adoring student gazing up in admiration and love at the wonderful teacher. As is clear from the use of the phrase elsewhere in the New Testament (for instance, Paul with Gamaliel), to sit at the teacher's feet is a way of saying that you are being a student, picking up the teacher's wisdom and learning from him. And in that very practical first-century world you wouldn't do this just for the sake of informing your own mind and heart, but in order to be a teacher, a rabbi, yourself.

Jesus and women evangelists

The first evangelist recorded in the New Testament was a woman with whom Jesus struck up a theological discussion. The story of the Samaritan woman at the well (John 4:1–42) involved not only a woman but a Samaritan woman. We all know how the Jews felt about the Samaritans – verse 9 spells it out: "Jews didn't associate with Samaritans." But not only that, this woman was a

Samaritan woman who had had multiple husbands and was in an acute moral dilemma, evidence of her own victim status in a world where men held all the rights and women lived at their disposal. Rather than majoring on the sin of living together Jesus understood that the situation the woman was in was less about sin and more about being sinned against. This is a phrase that Catherine Booth used to describe prostituted women, in her work among them. She understood the Church's view of the life of a prostitute as one of sin. But, after having heard story after story of injustice, she clarified that the women she had met who had found themselves as prostitutes were much more sinned against than sinning. We see this attitude in Jesus a lot. He looked beyond the obvious religious sentiment to find the root causes of injustice and situations that tell us much more about the sickness of sin. Gender injustice is a deeply rooted sin sickness.

Jesus invites the Samaritan woman into a conversation about worship and admits to her that He is the Messiah. This confession of Jesus' true calling (John 4:26) is not found anywhere else yet in his public ministry. He gives this startling good news to a Samaritan woman in supposed moral (or at least religious) trouble. Wow! Even the disciples were uneasy when they returned and saw Jesus in this apparently compromised situation. Actually, they were just "surprised to find him talking with a woman" (John 4:27).

The woman immediately responds to what Jesus has

said to her by telling others about it. This is the classic definition of an evangelist: someone who shares the good news. The Samaritan woman brings the whole town to Jesus through the witness of her encounter with him. Scripture tells us that "Many of the Samaritans from that town believed in him because of the woman's testimony" (John 4:39). The conversion of these people by and through a woman evangelist is hard to believe given the cultural norms at the time. Technically, Jesus shouldn't have even spoken with her – that's how culturally oppressive her situation was. Clearly, this good news of a new kingdom was going to uproot the existing powers. Now, this gospel story – the one that empowers women and liberates them with the good news to use their gifts to change the world – now, that gospel has power!

Throughout the New Testament, women were often the first to hear good news, and were intimately concerned with bringing about its fulfilment. Think about the song that Mary sung when she knew that she would conceive and that God's kingdom would come through her (Luke 1:46–55). The revolutionary nature of her song still rings across the globe today. Calling believers to recognize the very nature and plan of God to uproot the systems of injustice and oppression, and to release, equip and empower the "weak" to overthrow the "strong". That's a beautiful vision.

Bible scholar and Church historian Susan Hyatt points out that

... the women were the last ones to leave the cross and the first ones to arrive at the Tomb (John 20:1–18; Matthew 28:1–10). When Mary Magdalene visited the tomb early Resurrection morning and found it empty, without delay, she reported back to the disciples that Jesus' body was missing. They all hastened to the scene, but they did not grasp the significance of the empty tomb because *"they still did not understand from Scripture that Jesus had to rise from the dead"* (John 20:9). So they returned home, but Mary lingered behind. It was then that Jesus appeared to her and said, "Go and tell my brothers…"

[Jesus' appearance to and commissioning of Mary] are significant for several reasons. During the forty days between His resurrection and ascension, Jesus appeared to His disciples at various times, and on one occasion He appeared to over five hundred of His followers. The Gospel writers, however, are explicit in noting that it was Mary Magdalene to whom He appeared first after his Resurrection. The importance which the evangelists attach to this fact indicates that it was not an accidental occurrence, but that Jesus purposely appeared first to this woman. He could just as easily have appeared to a man; instead, He honored a woman.[6]

The first person to whom He revealed himself as the risen saviour was a woman. Susan Hyatt observes, rightly, that actions speak louder than words. She points out that when Jesus appeared to Mary Magdalene, He was not just telling His disciples that women were important: He was showing them by His actions. Jesus made His intention even more clear by instructing her to "go and tell my brothers" (John 20:17).

This constitutes Mary's commission. She was specifically sent, by Jesus, to tell the other disciples the news of His resurrection – thus fulfilling the function of an apostle (literally, "one who is sent"). Mary, arguably, received the first apostolic commission from the Risen Lord – and what a message.

Note too that Jesus was sending this astounding news, of His resurrection, to a group of men. Mary's commission was not limited to "women's ministry": yet, so often today, this is precisely what many gifted women face, having to exercise their gifts within such confines.

You may say I'm exaggerating, but I remember hearing an interview with Billy Graham about his daughter being the one with the gift of speaking. The interviewer made a quick comment about how that was unfortunate given the Southern Baptists' stand on women preachers. Billy agreed. So, instead of passing on his speaking ministry to the most anointed, gifted and qualified family member, he found someone else. Why? Because of a theology that says that women can't speak to men. Jesus wouldn't have agreed with his decision – no offense to Billy. Jesus chose to offend the sensibilities of the religious leaders when they were in the way of God's kingdom coming.

What a powerful example it would have been if Billy had considered the same kind of prophetic action when it comes to the proclamation of the gospel around the world today.

Are we so blinded by our own cultural prejudices that we're prepared to sacrifice the gospel message delivered with power, simply because the person delivering it is a woman?

Susan Hyatt reinforces the counter-cultural nature of Jesus' approach by commenting that:

> This was revolutionary thinking, indeed, for in both Roman and Jewish courts of law, the testimony of a woman was not permitted as evidence. By appearing to Mary Magdalene, Jesus was, therefore, cutting through any remnants of disdain and prejudice in His male disciples toward His female disciples. He no doubt was also teaching the women something revolutionary about their responsibility. Thus, Jesus declared his equal acceptance and expectation of women while also confirming their public responsibility as ministers of the New Covenant.[7]

This is still very important today. Many people suggest that we should just leave churches and other religions that hold prejudicial views about women alone. Why do we care? Aren't there women in these churches and those religions who hold to the same biased teaching and have the same theology? The example of Jesus is to confront prejudice with affirmative action. He chose women because they were gifted and able and obedient and willing but also *because they were women*. He did that to make a strong point to a dominant culture that there was another way to live.

The Church needs to rise up and be like Jesus again. One of the reasons Jesus chose to confront the prevailing attitude to women, most theologians agree, is because the theology that insisted on that kind of prejudiced behaviour tolerated even worse behaviour elsewhere. When the woman caught in adultery was brought before Jesus we understand that there was a man she was caught with but not brought forward… Why? Because the systemic prejudice against women had been so normalized by religious tradition that men were not held accountable when it came to sins against women.

In fact, Jesus put men and women on an equal footing in marriage and in divorce. He suggests that the system that Moses had instigated to deal with extreme circumstances within marriage was being abused regularly by men who simply wanted the legal right to dispose of their wives.

> Some Pharisees came and tested him by asking, "Is it lawful for a man to divorce his wife?"
>
> "What did Moses command you?" he replied.
>
> They said, "Moses permitted a man to write a certificate of divorce and send her away."
>
> "It was because your hearts were hard that Moses wrote you this law," Jesus replied. "But at

the beginning of creation God 'made them male and
female'. 'For this reason a man will leave his father
and mother and be united to his wife, and the two
will become one flesh.' So they are no longer two,
but one. Therefore what God has joined together,
let man not separate."

When they were in the house again, the
disciples asked Jesus about this. He answered,
"Anyone who divorces his wife and marries another
woman commits adultery against her. And if she
divorces her husband and marries another man, she
commits adultery."

Mark 10:2–12

To understand the power of Jesus' statement here, we
must remember that divorce was allowed in first-century
Palestine, but only the man could initiate it. He could
rid himself of his wife if she displeased him in any
way. According to Tucker and Liefeld (*Daughters of
the Church*, Zondervan, 1987) some rabbis considered
the size of a woman's bosom, or the fact that she had
bad breath, to be allowable considerations in a divorce.
She could also be divorced if she spoiled her husband's
dinner, talked too loudly, or wasn't pretty enough. She
was considered to be one of her husband's possessions,
of the same status as his oxen and his home, according to
the rabbinical interpretation of the tenth commandment
(Deuteronomy 5:21).

Under Jewish law, a man could never commit adultery

against his wife. But if a wife committed adultery against her husband, he had the right to send her away. She, on the other hand, was never allowed to choose to leave him.

In Mark 10:2–12, Jesus brings equality into marriage for the first time, giving the wife equal rights as well as responsibilities that she did not have before. He did this first by eliminating the idea of divorce, except for unfaithfulness (Matthew 19:9). He then brought equality another step further by introducing the idea that a man could commit adultery against his wife. Finally, He promoted equality by suggesting that the woman had the same right to divorce her husband that the man had. He covered an option that in reality did not exist at the time, just to affirm the status of women. Jesus taught that a woman wasn't an object or a possession to be used and abused, but was a valuable human being who could be sinned against.

It's part of the intrinsic nature of injustice that it spreads to other areas if it isn't confronted. So, what might have started as a small prejudice against women ministering in the temple or being teachers, turns into a prohibition against women going to school, which then develops into women being domestic slaves, and so on. Leaving an injustice alone in the hope that by doing so we'll save ourselves from divisions within the Church is not an option. We know from history that injustice will not simply be left alone. It'll grow and fester and bear fruit – and that fruit will be at the expense of the next generation. Do we want our daughters' lives to be limited and for them to suffer the abuse and prejudices we wanted out of? We don't have the time or the luxury simply to ignore a dangerous theology that leads to the oppression of women.

We have points to make.

We have a people to liberate.

It is not OK for churches to use the name of Jesus to spread hate and inequality and injustice around like it's the fragrance of Christ, when really it only smells like the world in all its various degrees of stink. The philosopher Edmond Burke said that "The only thing necessary for evil to triumph is for good people to do nothing."

Jesus and women in the image of God

Jesus strove in many ways to communicate the equal dignity of women.

Leonard Swidler points out that in one sense, these efforts culminated in Jesus' parable of the women and the lost coin, told in Luke 15:8–10. In this story, God himself is represented by a woman.

Jesus told this story, along with two others, to show the Pharisees and scribes how deeply concerned God is for everyone who is lost.

The first story was of a shepherd who left his ninety-nine sheep to go and look for the one that was lost. In this parable, the shepherd is God. In the third parable, about the prodigal son's return home, the prodigal's father is God. The second story, the one in the middle, is about a woman who looked for her lost coin. Clearly, in this story, the woman is God.

Jesus did not shrink from the notion of God as feminine. "In fact," Swidler comments, "it would appear that Jesus included this womanly image of God quite deliberately at this point, for the scribes and Pharisees were among those who most of all denigrated women – just as they did 'tax-collectors and sinners'."[8]

I know from reading some very stark reviews online that one of the big objections to the novel *The Shack* by William P. Young, that everyone and their dog read a few years ago, was the book's portrayal of God as a woman. This did strike me as odd, considering the comments above about Jesus choosing to describe God as a woman. And this isn't the only place where Jesus ascribes feminine attributes to God. Jesus says of himself that He's like a mother hen who longs to bring her chicks under the folds of her wings. The Holy Spirit has such feminine qualities that the early Church fathers used to refer to Holy Spirit as "she" and commonly thought of her as the feminine personality of the Godhead.

Jesus, women, and resurrection

There are accounts of three resurrections other than that of Jesus in the Gospels – and all of them closely involve a woman.

The raising of Jairus's daughter is related in three of the four Gospels: in Matthew 9:18–19, 23–26; Mark 5:22–24, 35–43 and Luke 8:41–42, 49–56.

Jesus also raised the only son of the widow of Nain from the dead, because "When the Lord saw her, He had compassion on her and He said to her, 'Do not weep'" (Luke 7:12–15) [ESV and NASB]. Widows were the lowest of all women. And a childless widow was the lowest of the low. Contemporary society had no compassion for these people. The religious establishment believed that a woman must have sinned very badly to suffer the judgment that led her to be in such a situation. The fact that Jesus saw her as a woman, with legitimate needs, and had compassion (deep feelings of love and empathy) for her, demonstrates that He valued her as a person. His response to her validated her pain for what it really was – the inevitable result of tragic circumstances, not pre-ordained judgment for some past sin. Jesus' decision to intervene and give her what she needed was a direct assault against a culture that would simply heap insult upon injury when it came to women in need. The religious leaders of that time would have gone out of their way to avoid the whole situation. This was mostly because contact with the dead brought about a whole heap of cleansing rituals that they would have to go through before they could re-enter the temple, but also because widows were supposed to be hidden away, not seen in public.

Finally, Jesus brought Lazarus out of the tomb at the request of the dead man's sisters, Martha and Mary. In this passage of scripture (John 11:1–43) it's clear that Jesus never shied away from an argument with women. The conversations He has with both Mary and Martha suggest that they were both His disciples. He listens to them, comforts them, cries, and then responds to their requests. He teaches them about God's kingdom through their brother and his relationship with himself. Jesus rebukes, calms, hears, answers, and teaches the two women – as a matter of fact, His relationship with both Mary and Martha is closely mirrored in his relationships with the rest of His disciples.

I'm pretty certain we haven't read about Jesus' ministry through this lens very much. We too often reduce Jesus' actions and attitudes to lovely spiritual principles that we try and live out, but we end up by denying their true practical power. If we are to ask ourselves what Jesus would do, then we must be prepared not just for some devotional, super-spiritual answer, but for the reality of a practical affront to the dominant culture.

Jesus wants to liberate women. All of them. Everywhere.

To understand this about Jesus is not to diminish Him

and His work, as some prejudiced folk would suggest. It is to embrace Him as He presented himself to be: Jesus, the feminist.

CHAPTER NINE

The Witness of the Holy Spirit

Catherine Booth used to say, "The Holy Spirit is the highest law." That belief was what fuelled The Salvation Army to encourage women to speak the gospel out loud and in public. Even when to do so was contrary to the cultural norms of the day, or against the actual law of the land. The Holy Spirit trumps evil. Every time.

This witness of the Holy Spirit follows the same pattern today as when the Spirit confirmed the work of the apostles in the early Church.

Peter experienced this in his dealings with non-Jewish believer Cornelius and his household (Acts 10). God had to teach Peter, through the Holy Spirit, a new way to live out the truth of the gospel. Peter had to lay aside all that his previous personal and cultural history had taught him, and follow God's new way of doing things. The barriers between Jews and non-Jews had been broken down, and Peter needed to act in the light of this. He experienced this new revelation through a mixture of prayer, scripture, experience, and reason. This same mixture is changing and transforming believers all over the world today. This is a revelation of the Holy Spirit – and we cannot resist it.

Both before and since Catherine Booth there have been other incredibly gifted and strong women speakers whom God has used very powerfully. Many female American revivalists were active in the "Great Awakenings" that swept the country. They all bore witness to God's desire to see women released to serve Him in their giftings.

But we have written these women evangelists out of history. According to theologian and historian Priscilla Pope-Levison,

> Despite their persistent presence on street corners and in churches, camp meetings, and public halls across the nation, the significant contribution of women evangelists to American religious life, past and present, has not been seriously considered. Simply put, women evangelists are a forgotten history. They are notably absent from histories of American evangelism, which routinely begin with Jonathan Edwards (1703–1758) and then continue the male trajectory through each generation, from Charles Finney (1792–1875) to Dwight Moody

(1837–1899) to Billy Sunday (1862–1935), to Billy Graham (1918 –)."[1]

All of these women had their gifts confirmed by the power of the Holy Spirit. And the Spirit confirmed their use of these gifts in public, to mixed audiences, as their preaching and teaching, their lives and their witness, bore fruit in the lives of their listeners. Many of these women's ministries are described by Pope-Levison. Here are a few examples.

Phoebe Palmer (1807–1874) came from a wealthy, committed Methodist family in New York. At the age of nineteen she married Walter Palmer, a homeopathic doctor, and the couple had four children. However, three of the four died in infancy, and Phoebe came to see this tragedy as God's punishment because she had neglected her religious duties.

In 1840, aged thirty-three, she took on the leadership of what became known as the Tuesday Meeting for the Promotion of Holiness. She developed her speaking skills, mainly at camp meetings, and as attendance grew – she attracted both clergy and laity from a variety of denominations – she started to travel alone while Walter stayed in New York, running both his practice and their household. From the 1850s the two travelled together, however, and their extensive itinerary included a four-year evangelistic tour of Great Britain. The British turned out in force to welcome her, and audiences in the thousands were not unusual.

Phoebe's gruelling schedule damaged her health,

and she would die prematurely at the age of sixty-six. Nevertheless, she found time to become involved in social work, founding the Five Points Mission in the slums of New York, which offered a chapel, schoolroom, rent-free apartments, and a variety of other social projects.

In addition to all this, she was also active as a writer, editing *The Guide to Holiness*, the journal of the growing holiness movement, and publishing several books on holiness and on the right of women to speak in public.

Julia Foote (1823–1900) was a black woman, born in New York to former slaves. Converted at the age of fifteen, she married a sailor, George Foote. The couple moved to Boston, where Julia joined an African Methodist Episcopal Zion (AMEZ) church. Here, despite opposition from her pastor and husband, she started to speak of her experiences of conversion and sanctification.

Although she was expelled by her congregation in 1844, she was convinced she had received a call from God to preach. She started to travel as an evangelist, speaking in communities across the northern United States. In 1851 she had to call a halt, needing to care for her invalid mother: she had also lost her voice, and would not speak again until 1869, when she experienced a divine healing. Setting out on the road once more, she attracted increasing congregations: an estimated 5,000 people came to hear her at a holiness meeting in Lodi, Ohio. Belatedly, her denomination came to acknowledge her ministry. She was the first woman to be ordained a deacon in the AMEZ

(1894) and only the second to be ordained an elder, shortly before her death in 1900.

Emma Ray (1859–1930) was born a slave, and raised in poverty in Missouri. She and her husband, L.P., made the long trek north and west to Seattle, seeking work, and soon after they arrived the pair were converted through the African Methodist Episcopal Church (AME). They would spend nearly thirty years ministering to the poor and homeless in the Seattle slums.

Emma, a gifted leader, enlisted fifteen women from her church and with them helped to found the Frances Harper Coloured unit of the Women's Christian Temperance Union, serving as its president. With her WCTU Unit, she paid regular visits to the town jail, holding services on Sunday afternoons, while on Wednesday afternoons she and another strong woman leader, Mother Ryther, who ran an orphanage in Seattle, would together visit prostitutes and hold services in local brothels.

For a brief period, from 1900 to 1902, Emma and her husband ran a mission in Kansas City, Missouri, for children living in poverty. The mission provided clothing and food, a warm place to gather in winter, and trips during the summer months, along with a weekly Sunday School.

In due course Emma and L.P. joined the Free Methodist Church, under whose auspices they were licensed as Conference Evangelists, preaching throughout Washington State. Emma's powerful testimony has survived her: "I was born twice, bought twice, sold twice, and set free twice. Born of woman, born of God; sold in slavery, sold to the devil; freed by Lincoln, set free by God."

Evangeline Cory Booth (1865–1950) was one of the children of William and Catherine Booth, who together founded The Salvation Army. Gifted, courageous and forthright, she was still in her late teens when she was assigned her own Army post in the London slums, earning herself the soubriquet "White Angel of the Slums". In swift succession she became Principal of the Army's Training College in London, then Army Field Commissioner for Great Britain, and then – still a young woman – Territorial Commissioner for Canada and Newfoundland.

In 1904 she was appointed to a still more demanding post: Commander of the American branch of The Salvation Army, whose headquarters were based in New York. She would hold this position for thirty years. In 1919 she received the DSM (Distinguished Service Medal) from President Woodrow Wilson on behalf of the Army, in recognition of the Army's contribution to the war effort by the "Sallies", the female Salvationists, whose heroic care of soldiers on the front line had won widespread admiration.

Evangeline had many gifts, not least as a fund-raiser: due in large measure to her efforts, the Army's first national fund-raising campaign collected $13 million.

Her last Army post, in a most distinguished career,

was as General of The Salvation Army at its International Headquarters in London, a step away from St Paul's Cathedral. From here she became the first woman – but not the last – to oversee the Army's work worldwide.

Ida Bell Robinson (1891–1946) grew up in Pensacola, Florida. Converted in her teens at a street meeting, she soon began leading prayer services in people's homes.

In 1909 she married Oliver Robinson, and the couple moved north to Philadelphia in search of work. Ida joined the United Holy Church of America, developing her speaking gifts by preaching on the streets. The UHC ordained her in 1919, appointing her to a small mission church, where her gifts as an evangelist and pastor were much appreciated.

However, the UHC proved increasingly stifling, and Ida came to the conclusion that the opportunities for women within its ranks were dwindling. This was a troubling realization, and she sought God's will in fasting and prayer. As a consequence she reached the conclusion that God was calling her out – to "come out on Mount Sinai", as she put it – so that she could be used to "loose the women".

This proved the birth of a new denomination, the Mount Sinai Holy Church of America. Of the nine founding members of the Board of Elders, six were women, as were all four of its top officers. Ida, a talented evangelist and church planter, set about her work with a will – she was consecrated bishop in 1925 – and at the time of her death in 1946 the denomination consisted of eighty-four churches. There were more than 160 ordained ministers, of whom 125 were women. In addition, the MSHC had established an accredited school in Philadelphia, mission work in Cuba and Guyana, and a farm in South Jersey which offered a safe haven away from the city.

❖ ❖ ❖

There are countless examples of women preachers around the globe today who are experiencing an incredible witness of the Holy Spirit through the fruit of their ministry. I've just returned from India where Joyce Myer packed out the Coliseum and spoke spiritual truths to hundreds of thousands of people in a land where women still struggle for practical freedom in everyday life. Most of them are still valued in "cow currency".

I first heard about Joyce from the leader of The Salvation Army in that region, who is a widow, but who rises up in the power of the Holy Spirit and offers strong leadership even in a culture that resists it. The Holy Spirit is witnessing for both of these women with great fruit as they exercise their gifts. God's kingdom is expanding through their efforts.

I have mentors who are strong women with tremendous Holy Spirit power, who speak God's word and bear incredible fruit for God's kingdom.

Patricia King, a prophet and preacher, has been

instrumental in modelling a godly life as a wife and mother, without compromising God's call to preach and evangelize.

Stacey Campbell was the first woman I met who modelled an itinerant preaching lifestyle while mothering five young children. Until I saw her example I still believed that for me to obey God in his calling to preach meant I'd be ruining my own children. This is another lie of the enemy. Catherine Booth (among many others) was an extraordinary mother at the same time as founding a movement and keeping up a gruelling preaching schedule.

When I was first converted, it was through the witness of a godly woman leader who exemplified love in a practical way. Then I was drawn to the dynamic stories of daring missionary women preachers and leaders who the Holy Spirit used with great power. Jackie Pullinger's story was among the most enthralling, and General Eva Burrows, world leader of The Salvation Army at the time, was of great encouragement to me – and still is. The irony of this was that I picked up many of these great classic missionary stories while I was on a mission trip with an organization that limited the role of women in the Church! The great hypocritical missionary reality of letting women lead "over there" but not "here" speaks of an even greater layer of prejudice and racial injustice.

Needless to say, I'm surrounded by mentors, peers, and friends who have gifts of evangelism and leadership, who are female and are examples to all believers. I esteem them and count it a great joy to be able to use my gift to be a part of this great army of women evangelists as we advance God's kingdom on earth.

CHAPTER TEN

A Deeper Look

Junia, a woman apostle

The highest leadership position in the Church is that of apostle, the head of the Church hierarchy since Bible times. Many Christians, particularly those who hold a complementarian position on women and women's roles, say that women can lead in a church, but can't be an apostle or the head of a church. This view runs smack into the person of Junia, who is listed as an apostle in the New Testament Church.

For many years many people thought that Junia(s) was a man, or, if they were prepared to admit that she was a woman, they discounted her as being just someone who happened to be highly regarded by the apostles, rather than being a woman who held a top leadership role in her church. But recent scholarship shows that she was both a female and an apostle!

Romans 16:7 says, "Greet Andronicus and Junias, my relatives who have been in prison with me. They are outstanding among the apostles, and they were in Christ before I was". The New American Standard and the NASU both use the word "outstanding", and the KJV uses "of note", meaning notable.

The *United Bible Societies Handbook Series*, an acknowledged authority composed of a board of respected translators, first acknowledges that the pair are a male/female team: "Andronicus and Junias… could easily have been husband and wife, or brother and sister." They acknowledge that some have misunderstood the sentence to mean "the apostles know them well", but a far more acceptable interpretation would imply that these two people were both counted as apostles, and were well known in that role.

Being an apostle is listed as one of the spiritual gifts given by God, and the ability to do the job is given by God himself: "And in the church God has appointed first of all apostles, second prophets, third teachers, then workers of miracles, also those having gifts of healing, those able to help others, those with gifts of administration, and those speaking in different kinds of tongues" (1 Corinthians 12:28).

In all the passages that explain spiritual gifts (how they are given, and how they should be used) there is no indication whatsoever that such gifts are limited to men. The whole thrust of the Bible's teaching is that men and women should work together, using such talents and abilities as they have received to serve God's people and to grow God's kingdom. Diana D. McDonnell[1] makes it clear that since Junia received this highest spiritual gift – that of an apostle – along with her husband Andronicus, it is obvious that a woman can also be called to service as a prophet, teacher or any other role that requires the exercise of spiritual gifts.

Women in church

The intricate realities of biblical exegesis are hard to understand sometimes, especially when our culture has been teaching us something different for years. Our prejudices can distort our perception. So here's a recap for you of the main views about the interpretation of 1 Corinthians 14:26–37, which deals with women speaking in church.

The TNIV translates the passage like this:

What then shall we say, brothers and sisters? When you come together, each of you has a hymn, or a word of instruction, a revelation, a tongue or an interpretation. Everything must be done so that the church may be built up. If anyone speaks in a tongue, two – or at the most three – should speak, one at a time, and someone must interpret. If there is no interpreter, the speaker should keep quiet in the church; let them speak to themselves and to God.

Two or three prophets should speak, and the others should weigh carefully what is said. And if a revelation comes to someone who is sitting down, the first speaker should stop. For you can all prophesy in turn so that everyone may be instructed and encouraged. The spirits of prophets are subject to the control of prophets. For God is not a God of disorder but of peace – as in all the congregations of the Lord's people.

Women should remain silent in the churches. They are not allowed to speak, but must be in submission, as the law says. If they want to inquire about something, they should ask their own husbands at home; for it is disgraceful for a woman to speak in the church.

Or did the word of God originate with you? Or are you the only people it has reached? If any think they are prophets or otherwise gifted by the Spirit, let them acknowledge that what I am writing to you is the Lord's command.

Verses 34 and 35, which refer to women remaining silent in churches, are the difficult ones.

Some commentators say that Paul is simply contradicting himself in these verses, compared to his other statements about worship, and although he's a bit confused, he must still be right. Women are not meant to speak in church and should always cover their heads. I actually sat beside one woman at an event who, when it was time to pray, felt that she had to use her napkin to cover her head for fear of breaking this scripture – and the only napkin she had to hand was a dirty one! But to believe this view means believing that Paul is schizophrenic, or at least has conflicting views, because he is being inconsistent with what he has just instructed about orderly worship. We know that these instructions were for the whole church – including women.

The second theory is that Paul never said this at all. Some expositors believe that these versus are so unlike what Paul says elsewhere that they must have been inserted during the translation from Greek to Latin. Many of these commentators would like to insert a footnote explaining that these verses cannot be found in the earliest manuscripts.

Another explanation (and an explanation is required for these two verses) is that the way that early worship was conducted most likely required some instruction. The set up in the early churches was that men and women sat in separate sections. So, if a woman was confused about what was going on in church and tried to ask her husband, it would require her shouting over the rest of the crowd towards the section where the men sat. Because society didn't educate women, there may have been many times where women caused disturbances during the worship or teaching, in order to ask questions. Paul is simply trying to solve a practical problem in the local church.

The best theory, considering the unlikely nature of the first theory, the problematic issues around the second, and the guesswork of the third is this: the passage is simply missing some quotation marks. In this passage (and indeed in the whole of his letter to the Corinthians) Paul is refuting the Judaizers. These were people who were trying to use the law to push the New Testament Christians into having to keep to all the traditional religious rules and regulations, which would restrict their freedom and confuse them about what it meant to be saved. Now, when Paul says "as says the law", he is *not* quoting from the Old Testament, although that's what "the law" would usually mean. So, most expositors suggest that he is referring to the oral law, which is what the Judaizers were using to confuse both the Gentiles and the new Christians. People who hold to this theory suggest that in verses 34 and 35 Paul is quoting the teaching of a popular rabbi – a teaching that Paul then proceeds to debunk. This makes the most sense in light of the context, the larger witness of scripture, and Paul's other words and letters. It also makes more sense of the words directly following the quote, which sound much more like a rebuke than an instruction.

If you'd like to know more about this, look up the articles "Did Paul Really Say, 'Let the Women Keep Silent in the Churches'?" by Dennis J. Preato, and *Covet to Prophesy* by Katharine Bushnell, both on www.godswordtowomen.org.

Another controversial passage about women in church is found in 1 Timothy 2. In the NIV it's headed, "Instructions on Worship".

> I urge, then, first of all, that requests, prayers, intercession and thanksgiving be made for everyone – for kings and all those in authority, that we may live peaceful and quiet lives in all godliness and holiness. This is good, and pleases God our Saviour, who wants all men to be saved and to come to a knowledge of the truth. For there is one God and one mediator between God and men, the man Christ Jesus, who gave himself as a ransom for all men – the testimony given in its proper time. And for this purpose I was appointed a herald and an apostle – I am telling the truth, I am not lying – and a teacher of the true faith to the Gentiles.
>
> I want men everywhere to lift up holy hands in prayer, without anger or disputing. I also want women to dress modestly, with decency and propriety, not with braided hair or gold or pearls or expensive clothes, but with good deeds, appropriate for women who profess to worship God.
>
> A woman should learn in quietness and full submission. I do not permit a woman to teach or to have authority over a man; she must be silent. For Adam was formed first, then Eve. And Adam was not the one deceived; it was the woman who was deceived and became a sinner. But women will be

kept safe [or saved] through childbearing – if they
continue in faith, love and holiness with propriety.

With passages like this there must be an explanation that
makes sense of the larger context and the whole weight of
scripture. I don't mean that we should try to explain away
difficult passages so that they say what we want them to
say, as if we were trying to tickle our ears. But we do need
to get at their real meaning.

For a start, it's worth pointing out that Paul brought
Priscilla as well as her husband Aquila to Ephesus to serve
in a teaching capacity (Acts 18), and made significant use of
women in his ministry. He hailed several women as fellow-
labourers in the gospel (Romans 16:1–15; Philippians
4:2–3) and asked the Church to submit to women like
these (1 Corinthians 16:16). It was Paul who made the
wonderful statement that in Christ there is neither male
nor female, and said that before the Lord there is neither
man without the woman nor woman without the man
(Galatians 3:28; 1 Corinthians 11:11f.).

How can these actions and attitudes be reconciled
with the text in 1 Timothy? And what should we make
of the doctrine that women must continue to bear the
responsibility for the sin of Eve? How does this line
up with Christ's full and perfect atonement for sin and
with the biblical teaching that the child shouldn't be held
accountable for the parent's sin (Deuteronomy 24:16; 2
Chronicles 25:4; Jeremiah 31:29f.; Ezekiel 18:20)? And
then there's the matter of salvation through childbearing:

how does this fit with the New Testament's resounding affirmation of salvation by faith?

In order to make sense of all this, we need to start by looking at the context. There are some signs in the letter that it was sent to Timothy while he was in Ephesus. And one of the main things we know about religion in Ephesus at that time is that the dominant religion in the city, with the biggest temple and the most famous shrine, was a female-only cult. The temple of Artemis (that's her Greek name; the Romans called her Diana) was a massive structure that dominated the whole area; and, as befitted worshippers of a female deity, the priests were all women. They ruled the show and kept the men in their place.

Now, if you were writing a letter to someone in a small, new religious movement with a base in Ephesus, and wanted to say that because of the gospel of Jesus the old ways of organizing male and female roles had to be rethought from top to bottom, you might well want to avoid giving the wrong impression. One of the features of the new way of doing things was that women were to be encouraged to study, and learn, and take leadership roles. So was the apostle saying, people might have wondered, that women should be trained up so that Christianity would gradually become a cult like that of Artemis, where women did the leading and kept the men in line? That, it seems to me, is what 1 Timothy 2:12 is denying.

N. T. Wright points out that Paul is saying, like Jesus in Luke 10, that women must have the space and leisure to study and learn in their own way, not so that that they can muscle in and take over the leadership as in the Artemis cult, but so that men and women alike can develop whatever gifts of learning, teaching and leadership God is giving them.

Another important fact about the actual translation of the scripture itself is that the Greek verb translated in the twelfth verse as "have authority over them" is so unusual that it only occurs once in the whole Bible. This word, *authentein*, seems to have overtones of being bossy or seizing control. It's usually translated as "to bear rule" or "to usurp authority", yet a study of other Greek literary sources reveals that it did not ordinarily have this meaning until the third or fourth century – well after the time of the New Testament.

So what did it mean? Research by Catherine C. Kroeger suggests that the word *authentein* originally had a sexual and murderous meaning and may be connected with the cult of Artemis. The women who followed this cult were taught a lot of heresies including the idea that sexual intercourse was a way of connecting with the divine. So this popular religion encouraged women to be seductive and sexually licentious as part of their worship. Temple prostitution was an everyday reality. If the word *authentein* in the context of 1 Timothy refers to sexual behaviour, it puts a quite different interpretation on the entire passage.

Obviously, the sexual practices of the main cultural

religions were affecting the Church. The Gnostics (who taught that the physical world doesn't really matter much at all) fuelled this way of thinking by suggesting that sexual intercourse had a mystical, divine aspect.

We know by the content of the other New Testament letters, which include instructions for the early Church in Asia Minor (such as Revelation 2:20 and 2 Peter), that false teaching about sexual immorality was a major issue. It had had such an effect that in some churches the communion love feast sometimes turned into an orgy!

So a translation along the lines of "I forbid a woman to teach or engage in fertility practices with a man" would make sense, implying that women (perhaps women who were formerly members of the Artemis cult) should not involve men in a heretical kind of Christianity which encouraged licentious behaviour.

The biblical scholar Dr David H. Scholer comments that, "the evidence clearly and strongly supports the view that *authentein* carries almost exclusively a negative meaning in Paul's Greek context, which would support the idea of 'domineer', 'usurp', or some such translation. Consequent upon this, the case is very strong on the basis of this term alone that 1 Timothy 2:8–15 is addressing a particular problem of abuse in the church, undoubtedly related to the false teaching/teachers opposed in 1 and 2 Timothy."[2]

So how do these issues of translation and context affect our reading of 1 Timothy?

Well, for one thing, the context of verse 12 fits well with general instructions as to how women should dress (modestly) and the head-covering bit fits in with the fact that the temple prostitutes of Artemis didn't cover their heads. Paul is instructing the church that they shouldn't look like the Artemis cult. They are to be distinguished by modesty and submission to one another. The letter is written to correct an imbalance, which makes sense in its context.

Going on in the chapter to verse 15, with its reference to salvation through childbearing: this might refer to the fact that, in those days, a woman's social and economic salvation came about through being married and having a family. Or it might reflect concern for the welfare of children who were brought into the world as a result of immoral practices.

An inevitable result of the sexualized worship practised by members of the Artemis cult was the birth of illegitimate and uncared for children. These were often raised in the temple as child prostitutes and faced a lifetime of sexual servitude. This reality makes marriage and family and having children a life-saving reality for the women and the men living in such extreme situations. This is also the way God had designed children to be born and raised, within the context of marriage. Far from being a sentence of subjection to male domination, this teaching presented the option of family to many women who had previously only known sexually predatory behaviour.

Finally, it's well worth pointing out that the ministry restrictions placed on women in 1 Timothy 2 aren't based on the creation order. They are based in the story of the temptation. Although in verse 13 Paul comments that Adam was formed first, then Eve, he doesn't draw any conclusion from this order. The point that he goes on to make is that Adam wasn't deceived, but Eve was, and she became the first transgressor (verses 13–14).

Adam had been instructed by God about the prohibition to do with the tree of the knowledge of good and evil before Eve existed. For this reason, Eve was less prepared than Adam to face the tempter. Adam himself was present during the temptation episode, but he remained silent (Genesis 3:6). Despite Eve's disadvantage, she boldly engaged the tempter and she was the one who became deceived.

Dr Bilezikian comments that this illustration from the Genesis temptation story has nothing to do with assigning all women, of all times, a subordinate status in church life. Adam and Eve had joint responsibility to populate the earth and be stewards of the created order (Genesis 1:28). These joint mandates were given to both Adam and Eve. There was no distinction between their two roles, in terms of their gender. To undertake these tasks, man and woman must have been expected to work together, bringing together their best abilities. They were equal partners, complementing each other.

The reason Paul cited this passage was to make the

point that those who are untaught, or unqualified, should not aspire to teaching functions, or expect to become leaders. Their first charge is to sit quietly and learn (1 Timothy 2: 11–12).[3]

CHAPTER ELEVEN

A Love that Empowers

Some people suggest that I should just lighten up and let people believe the doctrine of authoritarian male headship in marriage if it works for them... But the reality is far too damaging for me to do that. After all, say many men and women, headship works for us. Well, the problem isn't just a pragmatic one. It's of theological importance. It's about how we view God.

See, marriage was always meant to be a reflection of God. A godly marriage is meant to display love. God is love. As we've mentioned before, the Trinity is this wonderful expression of mutually submitted members of a community who love each other deeply. No one needs to be in charge – what is clear is their love for one another.

That should be enough.

Terrible injustice is suffered at the hands of well-meaning men and women because of false beliefs around the roles of women and men within marriage.

It's time to talk truth.

I've just finished reading an incredibly interesting article about marriage by a Christian counsellor and research specialist. He emphatically rejects the traditional headship model of marriage for several reasons. One is a true reading of scripture. The other is the reality of traditional marriages and the unhappiness of the people within them.

Among all religious people, of all faiths, practising Jews and born-again Christians have the highest divorce rates, at 30 per cent and 27 per cent respectively. Nominal Christians follow them at 24 per cent. Even more revealing and disturbing is the finding that atheists and agnostics have the lowest incidence of divorce at 21 per cent.

Why is this? Spokesperson Ron Barrier for American Atheists offers some reasons why he thinks this is so. Dennis Preato quotes him as saying that "Atheist ethics are of a higher calibre than religious morals, and with atheism, women and men are equally responsible for a healthy marriage. There is no room in Atheist ethics for the type of 'submissive' nonsense preached by Baptists and other Christian and/or Jewish groups. Atheists reject, and rightly so, the primitive patriarchal attitudes so prevalent in many religions with respect to marriage."[1]

This is incredibly interesting considering the mantra of those who hold to traditional views, which suggests that traditional marriages are the best way to live and the headship principle is God's design for marriage. Traditionalists claim that their view "should find an echo in every human heart". The root problem in marriage, they say, is the unwillingness of each partner to accept the role for which he or she was designed. If these traditionalists' statements were true, then marriages based on hierarchical relationships should be the happiest and most intimate of all marriages and have the lowest divorce rate. Yet born-again evangelical Christians have the highest divorce rate in the religious community.

Ephesians 5:21–33 says:

Submit to one another out of reverence for Christ. Wives, submit to your husbands as to the Lord. For the husband is the head of the wife as Christ is the head of the church, his body, of which he is the Saviour. Now as the church submits to Christ, so also wives should submit to their husbands in everything.

Husbands, love your wives, just as Christ loved the church and gave himself up for her to make her holy, cleansing her by the washing with water through the word, and to present her to himself as a radiant church, without stain or wrinkle or any other blemish, but holy and blameless. In this same way, husbands ought to love their wives as their own bodies. He who loves his wife loves himself.

After all, no one ever hated his own body, but he feeds and cares for it, just as Christ does the church – for we are members of his body.

For this reason a man will leave his father and mother and be united to his wife, and the two will become one flesh. This is a profound mystery – but I am talking about Christ and the church. However, each one of you also must love his wife as he loves himself, and the wife must respect her husband.

It's true to say that some people abuse or misconstrue the concept of authority in marriage. Traditionalists claim that because the man or husband is referred to as the head of a woman or his wife, this means that he is in charge over her (1 Corinthians 11:3; Ephesians 5:23). They miss the whole point that husbands are commanded to love their wives sacrificially (Ephesians 5:25). Husbands are not commanded to be in authority over their wives. Even the early Greek church exegetes and theologians tell us that the head metaphor (the word is *kephale*) means "source of life", or "origin", not "authority".

Kephale, translated "head", is what causes all the fuss. Dr David H. Scholer puts it this way:

> Whatever *kephale* might precisely signify in Ephesians 5:21–33, the context makes it clear that it carries for those in Christ no authoritarian sense for men. The opening sentence (5:21 NRSV) is the theme of the passage: "Be subject to one another out of reverence for Christ." In addition,

husbands are three times commanded to love their wives, an injunction that was not typical in first-century Mediterranean cultures. This injunction is explicitly modeled on Christ's relationship to the church, which is described totally and only in terms of self-giving activity. Thus, what Christ is to the church is the archetype for behavior within the believing community – subjection to one another out of reverence for Christ, a wife's submission to her husband as to the Lord, and a husband's love for his wife.

The use of the term *kephale* in the New Testament texts about the relationship of men and women, understood in their own contexts, does not support the traditionalist or complementarity view of male headship and female submission as described by those authors noted earlier. Rather, this data supports a new understanding in Christ by which men and women are viewed in a mutually supportive, submissive relationship through which either men or women can bear and represent authority in the church.[2]

Paul's discussion on marriage begins in Ephesians 5:21 where all Christians are invited to voluntarily submit to one another. But his only mention of authority in marriage is found in 1 Corinthians 7:3–7, where Paul gives husbands and wives mutual authority over one another's bodies.

Scholer concludes:

I am fully convinced that the Bible does not

institute, undergird, or teach male headship and female submission, in either the traditionalist or complementarian forms of evangelical thought, which exclude women from equal participation in authority with men within the body of Christ, whether in ministry or marriage or any other dimension of life. Rather, the Bible affirms, supports, and teaches by precept and example a mutuality or equality in Christ for women and men, both in ministry and in marriage. This is what is rightfully called evangelical feminism, although I fully realize that the term "feminism" creates conceptual and emotional difficulties for some people.

Because the Bible, and in particular the New Testament, affirms, supports, and teaches a genuine mutuality and equality in Christ, I believe this position should actively, even aggressively – in the Pauline sense of gospel obligation – be taught and acted upon in the church. This requires commitment and understanding, sensitivity and patience, love and forgiveness, humility and courage.[3]

This may be difficult to understand, because of our previous perceptions – perceptions that were largely created through our own prejudice, or through the prejudice of theologians and church leaders, some deliberately, but most ignorantly. This has resulted in us simply missing the larger gospel picture.

I've talked to so many people who say that ultimately someone has to have the final word in marriage – and that

God says that that person should be the man. This is a pragmatic argument, not really based on scripture.

And it simply isn't true. Not scripturally, and not practically. The final word on any subject shouldn't be left up to a specific gender, simply because they are man or a woman. The final word should be left to the person most qualified to make the decision.

In a marriage that is truly biblical this is about submitting our wills to God, praying together and then coming to a decision together, based on the needs, desires and wisdom of the whole family. In some families, decisions about finances could rest with the woman, who also happens to be an accountant. And in other families, decisions about what appliances to buy would rest with the man – if he is qualified to judge.

The point is not who is in charge, but what does love look like? Not a whimsical love where the husband is in charge but chooses to buy flowers to display affection – but a strong, honest, and true love, where each person in the relationship submits to the well-being of the other... for the benefit of God's kingdom. This kind of marriage will result in a lot more people understanding what God is like. Not only will people be liberated to exercise with freedom their gifts and abilities within the family unit, and then in the larger Christian community, but this kind of marriage will reflect the nature of God through our relationships with each other. Instead of the world looking at Christian relationships and seeing oppressive, dictatorial, and gender-biased roles, limiting potential and robbing people of genuine fulfilment, they'll see a sacrificial and loving empowerment. A love that wants the best for each other, regardless of cultural norms. A love that defies patriarchy. A love that isn't reactionary, but is proactive... a love that attracts.

Now, that would be a godly marriage.

CHAPTER TWELVE

What Liberation Looks Like

I know women who used to work in brothels who are now clean, free, and contributing good things to the world. Amazing women.

I know other women who are fighting for their rights and speaking out when the whole world seems to be telling them to be quiet. They're not listening.

I know other women who grew up in oppressive religious environments who have bravely stepped out of those systems and restrictions in order to use their God-given gifts for God's kingdom come. And it is. It is coming.

Liberation looks different depending on your perspective. If you are the enemy it looks terrifying, because it's the symbol of your final defeat. If you are an insecure man who has hidden behind cultural beliefs to protect his power and position, it looks threatening. You resist it because it confronts your own issues. If you are a woman who has accepted this "truth" as God-given fact and have based your whole life on its principles, this is hard. To revisit your life and your decisions in the light of liberation is a hard journey. But it's a worthy one.

I've written this book for all kinds of people. But mostly I've written this book out of submission and obedience to God. I've written this book because I've dedicated my life, my skills, my passion, my voice, my life for His kingdom to come. And His kingdom coming looks like freedom, liberty, equality, dignity, and empowerment for everyone. Galatians isn't just a nice idea – it's the reality of how God wants the world to be. It's pre-sin; it's Eden restored.

It's time to listen to Jesus and be the salt and light needed in the world. It's time to stop the gendercide, to rise up and be God's voice in the world, telling every young girl that she was created in the image of God. That she is worthy of respect and of nurture and of life in all its fullness. She was not born to be a slave. If it was for freedom that Christ set us free, then let's be free.

In our churches, let's challenge the structures that are based on faulty translations and poor exegesis.

In all our systems and structures, let's raise our voices and declare a new standard of equality for everyone.

In our marriages, let's celebrate the true concept and reality of marriage as love on display through mutual submission and respect.

In politics, let's demand the fair treatment of women and girls around the globe and take the issue of their liberation seriously.

In our hearts, let's allow the Holy Spirit to challenge, to stir, to rebuke, to correct, to instruct, to liberate, to comfort, to change... Let's change our mind about the things that limit God's work in us and embrace the revelation of God. Let us do this through his Holy Spirit, which seeks to set us free.

I'm seeking these conclusions: changes to structures, systems, denominations, marriages, politics, and hearts. It's a big ask.

But it's time to celebrate the liberating truth.

Notes

Chapter One

1. N. T. Wright, Paul for Everyone, p 23.

Chapter Two

1. Debbie Howlett, *USA Today*, http://www.usatoday.com/news/sept11/2001/10/17/afghan-women.htm
2. Barbara Kay, *National Post*, http://network.nationalpost.com/NP/blogs/fullcomment/archive/2010/03/26/barbara-kay-the-burka-not-worn-but-borne.aspx
3. Nicholas D. Kristoff and Sheryl WuDunn, *Half the Sky: How to Change the World*, Virago, 2010.

Chapter Three

1. Nicholas D. Kristoff and Sheryl WuDunn, *Half the Sky: How to Change the World*, Virago, 2010.

Chapter Four

1. Nicholas D. Kristoff and Sheryl WuDunn, *Half the Sky: How to Change the World*, Virago, 2010.

2. See www.godswordtowomen.org/ezerkenegdo.htm

3. www.crivoice.org/enumaelish.html

4. For more information about the work of this organisation see www.stopthetraffik.org

5. http://www.unhchr.ch/huricane/huricane.nsf/0/C7D6D222153 9FE18C125758300385FF8?opendocument

Chapter Five

1. Anna and Ryan Snyder, "When we said 'I do': One couple shares the story of their egalitarian wedding" in *Mutuality: the voice of Christians for Biblical Equality*, Vol 17, Issue 1, Spring 2010.

2. http://www.ntwrightpage.com/Wright_Women_Service_Church.htm

Chapter Six

1. See www.godswordtowomen.org/covet.htm

2. www.godswordtowomen.org/preato2

3. www.godswordtowomen.org/bilezikian

Chapter Seven

1. www.billygraham.org/articlepage.asp?articleid=1172

2. http://www.ntwrightpage.com/Wright_Women_Service_Church.htm

3. www. godswordtowomen.org/feminist

4. www.godswordtowomen.org/bilezikian.htm

Chapter Eight

1. www.godswordtowomen.org/feminist

2. www.godswordtowomen.org/alei.htm

3. www.godswordtowomen.org/feminist

4. www.godswordtowomen.org/feminist

5. http://www.ntwrightpage.com/Wright_Women_Service_Church.htm

6. www.godswordtowomen.org/jesus.htm

7. www.godswordtowomen.org/jesus.htm

8. www.godswordtowomen.org/feminist

Chapter Nine

1. www.myhome.spu.edu/popep/profiles.html

Chapter Ten

1. www.godswordtowomen.org/juniamcdonnell.htm
2. www.godswordtowomen.org/scholer
3. www.godswordtowomen.org/bilezikian.htm

Chapter Eleven

1. www.godswordtowomen.org/preato
2. www.godswordtowomen.org/scholer.htm
3. www.godswordtowomen.org/scholer.htm

Bible Acknowledgments: